＊

A GARLIC
TESTAMENT

A GARLIC
TESTAMENT

Seasons on a Small New Mexico Farm

Stanley Crawford

Edward Burlingame Books
An Imprint of HarperCollins*Publishers*

HarperCollins books may be purchased for educational, business, or sales promotional use. For information, please call or write: Special Markets Department, HarperCollins Publishers, Inc., 10 East 53rd Street, New York, NY 10022. Telephone: (212) 207-7528; Fax: (212) 207-7222.

FIRST EDITION

Designed by Laura Hough

Library of Congress Cataloging-in-Publication Data
Crawford, Stanley G., 1937–
A garlic testament : seasons on a small New Mexico farm / Stanley Crawford.—1st ed.
    p. cm.
Includes bibliographical references.
ISBN 0-06-018207-5
    1. Garlic—New Mexico. 2. Garlic. 3. Farm life—New Mexico. 4. Truck farming—New Mexico. I. Title.
SB351.G3C73 1992
635'.09789—dc20   91-50442

---

92 93 94 95 96 MAC/HC 10 9 8 7 6 5 4 3 2 1

To Adam and Kate

". . . a small obscure business

to the outer world, but to

themselves how wide and deep

and crowded!"

—EDITH WHARTON

CONTENTS

CONTENTS

CONTENTS

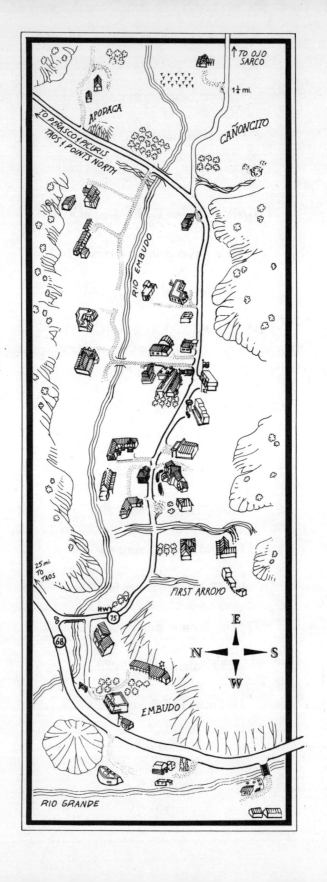

＊

ACKNOWLEDGMENTS

THE LABORS DESCRIBED within this book could not have been possible without the continual support of many friends and relatives over the past twenty years.

Those who helped Rose Mary and me build our house are too many to name, but most heroic by far were Jeff and Joan Carlisle, and Jon and Rhoda Carlisle, whose mud bricks of twenty years ago still hold.

No less tangible has been the continual support and encouragement of my parents, Helen I. and A. Bergman Crawford, and of Lorraine Pohlmann, and John and Lyn Pohlmann, and of Rose Mary's Australian family who have on many occasions extended us a hand from the other side of the world: Alice Klaphake, Zita, Ruben, and Van Klaphake, Don and Fran Wilton, and (almost family) Angus MacLaughlin.

Among those many who have been with us and for us on the farm for these many years, I would like to mention in particular: Susie Lucero, Alice Arellano, Ron and Nausika Richardson, Tom and Leti Seibel, Michael Meyer, Bob and Carolyn Grant, Lillian Maestas, and Charles Knoop.

For the book itself, I would not have met several

deadlines had not Lawrence Lucero irrigated the garlic fields over the course of two spring seasons—in addition to his usual work in the fields, the garlic shed, and on the transplanter.

Portions of this book were written at the MacDowell Colony of Peterborough, New Hampshire, and at the Centrum Foundation of Port Townsend, Washington, and with the support of a writing fellowship grant from the National Endowment for the Arts. Without such generous assistance the task would have been longer and far more difficult, and perhaps even impossible; and then I would not have known the steady and warm encouragement of Susan Bergholz and Kathy Banks.

El Bosque Garlic Farm
Dixon, New Mexico
August, 1991

*

I

AUTUMN:
PLANTINGS

1

GARLIC QUESTIONS
FINALLY ANSWERED

IN MY MOST RECENT novel the demented narrator claimed to have been the author of a number of horticultural pamphlets. He was most proud of one entitled "Garlic Questions Finally Answered." At the time he might have known more than I did. At the time I was unaware that relatively little had been published about garlic outside of specialized journals on the one hand and in places like the *National Enquirer* on the other, and I doubt I could have answered most of the "garlic questions" myself. In the fifteen years that have elapsed, the imaginary monograph became a private challenge to discover some of the puzzles of the plant, and particularly that not-so-common variety which circumstances have placed under my care.

What the author of "Garlic Questions Finally Answered" did not know, because he lived in a loveless world, was that if you grow good garlic people will love you for it. In fact, you can grow even fair garlic or even rather cosmetically inferior garlic, and people will still compliment you for your pains, more so than perhaps for any other vegetable crop.

There are several reasons for this. The most important

lies in the poor quality of most garlic sold commercially in the United States, most of the time, to judge from the complaints I receive from my own customers year after year. The following speech is a compendium of such complaints. It will be typically delivered by a middle-aged woman as I stand at the tailgate of my pickup, at the farmers' market in Santa Fe or Los Alamos, my wares spread out in lug boxes on plywood planks.

"I bought some garlic in the supermarket and it was no good," my customer will say. "It was all dried up. The bulbs were hollow. They were all moldy inside. There was nothing there. I had to throw it all out."

I have been on the receiving end of several hundred speeches in this vein about garlic purchased in supermarkets, a compassionate expression fixing itself upon my own middle-aged, weathered face as I lean against the back of my pickup. There are several ways to account for this state of affairs in a country known to be the world's largest producer of the crop, but I think that the greatest single factor lies in methods of national distribution. The American retail distribution system likes products that can be frozen, baked, freeze-dried, canned, shrink-wrapped, boxed up, strapped to pallets, warehoused, and shipped to the ends of the earth and back without undergoing noticeable deterioration.

Shelf life is one of the main products of our distribution system. But what's the shelf life of a garlic bulb? Three to six months, and six months will badly strain the outer limit. Which means that most of the garlic in most supermarkets from January to July has outrun its shelf life. Most of the garlic in the produce bins or in those little plastic packets from January to July is dying garlic, which is to say garlic that is beginning to rot or mold or else, having completed the process, is drying out.

[4]

From the point of view of the garlic bulb, the problem is that it wants to go back into the ground somewhere around October or November or December and to spend the winter there, where it's damp and cool and dark. The longer a bulb stays out in the air, and especially the dry air of a supermarket, the weaker it becomes. Ordinary plain air does not much nourish the bulb. Sprout inhibitors likely to have been sprayed on large commercial fields before harvest in order to keep the bulb from sending out roots and shoots probably do little to enhance the inner life of the bulb. Plastic packaging makes things not only worse but impossible—because the bulb does in fact need to breathe. Customers desperate to select a still-firm bulb will help squeeze the life out of the few viable cloves remaining. Oddly, what will be left often will be a quite handsome bulb, a bulb as light as a butterfly, a triumph of natural packaging over substance.

Garlic's natural winter home is in the damp, in the dark, in the cool, where it can send out roots to feed from the earth and prepare itself to resume growth in the spring. Which is what I have tried to explain, many hundreds of times, as customer and I stand both peering down into my lug boxes of garlic, in the dry summer air of northern New Mexico, under an implacable blue sky, imperceptibly drying out ourselves, our own shelf lives ticking slowly away.

"It'll keep forever in the ground," I finally suggest.

"Oh."

＊

2

UPRIGHTNESS IS ALL

IT SHOULD BE CLEAR by now that garlic grows in the ground. I mention this elementary fact because I have been asked so many times where it grows.

My particular ground, the specific "where," is a couple of bottomland fields in the narrow mountain valley of a tributary of the Rio Grande, elevation sixty-five hundred feet above sea level, latitude thirty-six degrees north of the equator.

In the more general where, the bulb reposes three to four inches beneath the surface, like other members of the lily family and most other bulbs, and stays in the ground from the time it is planted until it is harvested in the early summer. At my altitude garlic will spend most of its life under the ground, a good nine months of the year, and if the bulbs had their way they wouldn't come up for air at all.

So that when we put it back into the ground in the fall, back into its natural element, damp earth, its dark and cool home where it can resume the dream life of subterranean creatures, we are also putting a merciful end to its unnatural sojourn in the open air, on our shelves, in our baskets, and in our lethal plastic bags. The garlic bulb has of course learned to prepare for space travel with its layer upon

[6]

layer of brilliant white outer skin, its wrappers, its quadruple and quintuple wrappings, outer ones which enfold the entire bulb, with the innermost ones individually encasing the ten to twenty separate cloves the whole is partitioned into. And we have further trained it, bred it, cultivated it to prepare for its annual period of captivity in the atmospheric element out of the soil by somehow encouraging it to grow its white and shiny space suit, its heat- and light-reflecting skins, in order to hold in such moisture as it can bring along out of the earth, yet in order also to breathe as it must, as we all must.

"But," a newfound garlic friend will ask me one Saturday morning at the market in Santa Fe, as a crowd mills around our stand, while I am weighing and bagging, while Rose Mary is making change, while other voices are tugging at the sleeves of our attention. "But don't you need to place the cloves upright in the ground when you plant them?"

Consider a moment. That a plant that spends the greater part of the life cycle in the ground, a plant that has survived millennia of global mismanagement by mankind, that such a plant does not know at this late date which side is up? Uprightness is all. Break open your bulb of garlic, the one I have just sold you with a money-back guarantee, and peel an individual clove of its somewhat stiffer innermost skin, and then examine the yellowish-white flesh in the shape of a tangerine slice. There is a pointy tip, which the logic of growing things tells us is the top, and there is the root node, the germ, at the bottom. If the season is late and if the weather has been damp, or if the clove has been lying outside in a pile of leaves or old stalks, then the tip will have turned greenish and may even be sprouting the beginnings of a leaf, while the root node will be pushing out tiny nubbins or fingers that will soon become the silvery, translucent filaments of roots intending to fan out into the damp earth to gather nutrients and anchor the future plant.

Uprightness: we are told that it is one of the important tests of biological existence. At some point we learn to exclude mountains and certain rock formations as the necessary exceptions. Humans when they plant are almost always in a hurry. Or at least I am. Impossible to conceive of planting the thousands of cloves of even my modest garlic crop placed right side up, though there are farmers who have confessed, yes, they have planted their acre or so like that, individually, pressing each clove carefully right side up into the earth, herding a succession of wives and children and stepchildren into thoughts of an early grave. Nor can I conceive of a machine that could do so without damaging the cloves, a machine that could somehow pluck them out of a planter bin and place them a certain way in the earth, then cover them up without knocking them over. There's always something rough and tumble about planting—because with our clumsy implements we must reach from our atmospheric element down into another, down into the darkness of the soil. So despite our best efforts, or through indifference and haste, or because it doesn't matter, our garlic clove has landed upside down in the dark three or four or five inches below the surface, one fine morning at the end of September. Eventually the clove sprouts, and a leaf begins unsheathing itself in the general direction of Argentina or Japan, and the roots begin radiating out toward—to arrest the planet in a moment of time—Venus, Jupiter, or Mars. But obviously this can't go on very long.

It won't. Winter is coming. It will rain and snow. The soil will shift back and forth in structure from a rock-hard frozen state at one extreme to a granular mushy liquid at another. The roots of the clove will begin to grab hold. The single blade of leaf will turn toward warmth, toward light. The tangerine-slice shape of the clove will fill out and become olive-shaped, then almost perfectly spherical. From September or October until April, say, five months or so, the interactions of the growing bulb with the soil, which is freezing, thawing, moistening, drying, warming, cooling, interactions of an astounding mechanical complexity, will collectively favor uprightness in 90 percent of the cloves. By April, when serious leaf growth begins, the buffeting soil movements against the root-anchored sphere, with guidance from the rudder-like leaf growth blown in the spring winds above the surface, will have nudged our plant into triumphant uprightness, which is about as long as it takes a human baby to learn which way is up and how to get there. Which is to learn how to work both with and against the forces of gravity and local disturbances, like all living creatures.

＊

3

THE EARTH: THAT SEA

WHEN I FIRST STARTED out as a gardener, as a thirty-two-year-old trying to feed his family, I dug a little trench with a hoe and dropped in the cloves and covered them up and tamped down the earth with the hoe. I planted quite a few rows this way.

Then I bought a hand rototiller, the brand that apparently spends more money on advertising than it does on improving its product, and used that to prepare the ground to plant my garlic and other crops. I bought the machine from a friend who specialized in wearing out things faster than anybody else around. I got a couple of years of work from it until the transmission went out one summer day, in the middle of the half-acre field I was tilling. My cousin John was visiting from California at the time. The machine must have weighed over two hundred pounds. We pulled it out of the field by roping ourselves to it like draft animals and dragging it up the driveway to the shed.

Then I decided to get a tractor. Actually I already owned half of an old Farmall A that a friend and I had bought from the village postmaster, old Mr. Atencio. But my experiences with it were never satisfactory. Under my uncertain guidance its plows took forever to dig in at the end of each row, then dug in too far, plowing deeper and deeper until the machine stalled. The ailing pneumatic lift system which operated off the exhaust lacked a certain subtlety in raising and lowering the plow. The machine was also geared to the wide open fields of the plains, east of our mountains, not to the small two- and three-acre alluvial fields of a narrow mountain valley and soils that seemed to change in composition every twenty yards and were scattered with rocks.

To buy a new tractor I had to borrow money. The only people who might lend me some were the Farmers Home Administration. But I didn't own enough land for them to think of me as a farmer; I needed a couple of acres more, even to borrow for a small tractor. So I went to the bank and they surprised me by lending me some money to buy a couple of more acres. I borrowed the money and bought the land, then I went back to the FmHA and they said, Now we'll lend you your tractor money. All this took six months. I remember going to bed in a cold sweat night after night, for months on end, wondering how I could possibly pay off debts that had soared from almost nothing to eight thousand dollars.

It took me about ten years more to figure out that even an ingeniously designed Japanese tractor simply didn't automatically do everything just right and that it had its own special relations to gravity, soil, and myself. A young neighbor, also a recent immigrant from California, but one who had spent summers working on real farms and liked to sing on his tractor, probably told me more than I needed to know, and I probably pretended to listen carefully to his remarks and reflections while attempting to convert his multi-dimensional wisdom into some narrow cause-and-effect relation. But what I learned to do soon enough was to plant my garlic by making little furrows, two at a time, with some little cultivator shovel things that look like large and somewhat pointed horse's hooves, and then walking along and dribbling in the cloves so that they would fall more or less within a few inches of each other. Then I'd reset the same shovels, which are normally used for restoring irrigation furrows after cultivation, and get back on the tractor and run back up and down the rows and more or less cover up the garlic, with two such shovels set to each side of the twin planting furrows. This more or less worked for a couple of years. I spent an awful lot of time trying to figure out why rows gradually or suddenly got close together or far apart in some soil but not in others. But the problem wasn't the soil or the tractor or the implements, it was the way I was thinking.

You see a thing with wheels and you naturally think, It rolls. Tractors have wheels. They roll. Farming with a tractor is a matter of helping things roll back and forth. Or so it would seem. We do a lot of this as kids on carpets, or at least as a boy I did. I also did a lot of stuff with boats, in the bathtub, or the beach, or in streams in the mountains when we used to go camping. I used to make boats out of milk cartons by cutting them in half and floating them down the crystalline streams of the High Sierras, when I was a kid, when my parents took me camping. I could hardly wait for the next quart carton of milk with bright orange or red or blue lettering to be empty so I could cut it in half, make my way down to a wide, shallow trout stream, and sail my boat until the waxed carton finally became so waterlogged that the craft would sink and have to be thrown away. There was something about those cardboard boats bobbing among the smooth boulders, on the shallow water of the clear, chattering streams, that helped render the towering, soughing landscapes familiar and unthreatening. Others older and more powerful carved initials in trees, fished, shot deer and elk, but I sailed my little waxed carton boats and knew great happiness: images in memory that twenty years later would lure me back to such a stream where, within earshot, Rose Mary and I would build our house, raise our children, grow our garlic.

The relation of the tractor's implement to the earth is perhaps more akin to that of a hull to water than a wheel to earth, because what goes on below the surface is often more important than what takes place above it. A freshly plowed field, as you traverse it on a tractor, even feels like crossing rough water. When you plow, which I no longer do, or subsoil or rototill, which I do, you alter the structure of the soil in the direction of loosening it up, thereby aerating it, while subsequent operations, like furrowing, bedshaping, planting, and generally tramping about on it all serve to alter it back toward a more solid state. How your tractor behaves, how much traction it obtains, how it tracks, how the implements track, dig in, lift out, are functions of this and multiple other conditions, which include soil composition and moisture, rocks and organic matter, and the mood and intelligence and alertness of the creature manipulating the plastic-knobbed controls of the rear lift, throttle, gears. Learning this body of knowledge, which includes detailed mental maps of your gardens and fields and the topography of your own difficult temperament, can be the work of ten or more years for your New Age over-educated farmer with an M.A. in the Landscape of Ideas. Grow up on a farm, and the major problems can be the work of a few minutes; and you get to sing, too.

After ten years of working things like this out in the

wind and in the heat and in my dreams, I reached a new kind of crisis. I had come to northern New Mexico as a novelist, had stumbled into gardening, then into farming. I was much less of a writer, much more of a farmer. I had been pleased by this turn of events. As a writer who had been lucky in the early years of my career and who had had the luxury of about five clear years of writing time as a result, I had discovered that I was not the kind of writer who could turn out a book a year and make a sustained living at it—in fact, I was probably a poet who had miscast himself as a writer of narrative prose. Farming gave a kind of substance to my life. It was something I could talk freely about to other people, unlike my writing. It had other social dimensions as well. And it was gratifyingly physical.

Yet time passes. You begin to realize that soon your turn will come to grow old. You awake to certain facts. You're forty-eight years old, for example. What? Why so soon? You work yourself and your wife half to death each year, then have to borrow money to get through the winter, to cover your writing time, and then again in the spring to get the farm going again. And then if you're lucky you pay it all off, or some of it, in the fall, roll over what you can't, start all over again and hope for the best. You think you can keep this up the rest of your life? It depends on how you view the rest of your life, as long or as short.

This was five years ago. What I woke up to was the fact that I had slowly become more intelligent than my now relatively primitive equipment, even my little Japanese tractor, still youthful as a machine. Without being aware of the process I came to know how to do more than I had equipment for, I knew now that I was working harder than I needed to. At an age when it took an extra day to recover from overwork, I began to realize that physical labor was therapeutic only up to a certain point. I needed a bigger tractor, one that would not shake up the sediment in my kidneys every time I hit a bump; I needed about three kinds of planters, and a loader to lift the things that two hernia operations had told me I now had to be extremely careful with. I needed implements I knew existed somewhere, implements whose names and forms I was still in ignorance of but which I knew would serve me the next twenty or thirty years, the rest of my farming life.

The point of all this is to say simply that the way I now plant garlic is with a strange though mechanically comprehensible machine that I tow behind the tractor, a one-row transplanter on which have sat two at a time, variously, Rose Mary and our children Adam and Kate and assorted friends who have worked for us over the past five years. The machine plants a clove of garlic every five or six inches, more or less, three or four inches deep, moving along at about a mile an hour. Its two riders feed the scoops of a paddle-wheel-like device that carry the cloves down and drop them into the opened planting furrow. My business up front on the tractor is to drive in a straight line, adjust the depth of the transplanter, check for bolts and parts loosening or falling off, pass the time of day, think. Not unpleasant work, more accurate and less laborious though no faster than the old walking way; nor do my two riding planters find it onerous, though sometimes keeping up with the scoops is taxing.

And planting takes place at the peak of the autumn change, under clear blue skies, with the sun still high enough to warm the days, yet low enough that it seeks out the eye with its glintings. The tractor scarcely labors as it drags the machine through the soil, diesel engine rumbling away, while behind the transplanter scrapes and squeaks along, and cuts a deep crease, a vaginal opening in the moist dark earth, into which the twin riders, testicular in function, drop the white-skinned cloves, one at a time, one after another, hundreds by the row, thousands by the day.

＊

4

GARLIC GHETTOS

PLACE YOUR GENERIC garlic bulb on a table. I say generic because we won't get into distinguishing between garlic cultivars—cultivated varieties—for a while yet. Then crack it open the usual way by employing your opposed thumbs, and thumbnails, to pry open a fissure, which can then be enlarged with a slight twisting motion, in opposite directions, of your opposed wrists. The bulb should split in half.

Whether this is easy or difficult may tell you something of interest about your generic bulb, but again in a moment. With some additional twisting, prying, and abrading, you will soon be able to reduce the partitioned bulb into a heap of cloves surrounded by a debris of fine white skin. There are likely to be about fifteen cloves, though I have seen bulbs made up of as few as three or four.

You may also be in the presence of another component, which you will be tempted to brush aside or toss over to the garbage bin without further thought. Wait. Pick it up and have a look. The shape of a tiny umbrella or mushroom, though without much of a cap, what you are twirling around in your fingers is a stalk, possibly a seed stalk. At the top, or what is in fact the bottom end, there may even be a scraggly clump of dried roots. You may also have found just the root base, with some roots, and little or no stalk.

What you find will tell you whether you are in the presence of a bolting or top-setting cultivar or, more likely, a non-bolting type that does not send up a seed stalk or seed head. The vast bulk of garlic grown in this country is of the non-bolting type, and most of that will be sold under the category of California Early, which produces a larger, whiter-skinned bulb than California Late, whose darker-skinned bulb keeps longer. These are the two major commercial cultivars offered by the large suppliers of planting stock in Gilroy, California.

So let us assume your disassembled bulb is of the non-bolting type, California Early or Late or a close cousin. What you have just done is break up the bulb, which you would do to use it, or to plant it by digging a furrow in a newly prepared garden bed and placing the cloves six inches or so apart in the row.

In a state of nature, however, garlic bulbs do not possess the power to dig themselves up, break themselves apart into cloves, replant themselves in nice even rows. Garlic needs you and me for that. Garlic, like corn, though not quite as severely as corn, has been rendered evolutionarily vulnerable by the selective actions of millennia of cultivation—that is, the non-bolting types we're talking about. Garlic reproduces not sexually but by cloning, by dividing itself up like an amoeba. A bulb stuck in the ground forever, which is where I said it really wanted to be, will soon reach a dead end.

Let us go back to our garlic bulb on the table, before we broke it up, before we helped it complete its annual cloning process, though for this experiment we must make certain it's a non-bolting type, a type that does not send up a seed stalk, which is mostly what you see in the marketplace.

What we're going to do is not break it up, we're going to put it back into the ground as is, whole, unbroken up. The month is October, plus or minus sixty days. In the ground what will happen is that each of the cloves will decide that it's time for it to turn into an individual plant: each one will thus send out roots and send up a green point. Result: in the space that used to be occupied by one plant, now there will be ten or fifteen or twenty plants all vying for moisture, nitrogen, phosphorus, sulfur, and light.

What we've got is a garlic ghetto. We wait through the winter and the spring and the early summer and watch our little cramped and crowded garlic ghetto grow into a tight clump of leaves. Down below, in the ground, what's happening is that each of those cloves is not doing so well, they're not growing into nice plump bulbs. They're growing into cramped narrow bulbs with only a few cloves each, not the usual twelve or fifteen. Then in June or July, leaves and roots die back, as they should do, and the garlic ghetto falls into a state of dormancy that will last until October or so. Now what happens? We started out with fifteen cloves crammed into one small space. Now we have perhaps forty-five cloves crammed into about the same space, sardines into a can. Garlic thus crowded will produce a bulb with only three or four small cloves, not ten to twenty. And they only know how to grow up and down, not north or south, east or west, though they can somewhat swell themselves out in those directions. It's obvious that some of the cloves, maybe even most, are not going to make it. Unless a large animal takes to relieving itself often on the clump, our garlic ghetto is going to exhaust the surrounding soil. Now it's clear that it is better at maximizing potentials for disease and death than those of individual development and personal fulfillment—I speak from the point of view of the clove—and that it's lacking in opportunities for growth, advancement, evolutionary development, and transcendence of the garlic condition. Many of the cloves will not be able to grow large enough to store sufficient nutrients to carry themselves through the dormancy periods of summer and winter.

In short, it's clear that our garlic bulb of the non-bolting sort lives and thrives in the expectation of some kind of annual intervention that will lift it out of the ground, break it up into cloves, and replant it with improved spacing. Otherwise cloning, the annual cleaving of one into three to twenty segments, would not be a viable reproductive strategy. In other words, garlic as we know it today needs us as much as we need it. True, it would seem that the only way our garlic ghetto could have come into existence in the first place was as a long-term consequence of our monkeying around: it makes no sense for a plant in its right mind to put all its eggs into that kind of a basket, all by itself.

*

5

THE FLYING CLONE

THERE IS ANOTHER kind of garlic.

Back at the kitchen table, a random minority of you will have found a little umbrella- or mushroom-like seed stalk that marks the bulb as being a bolting or top-setting type. A taxonomy is not firmly established in these matters, but I have seen the terms "rocambole" and "serpent garlic" used as much as any. "Top-setting garlic" is the term I prefer. The outer skin may be streaked with purple, and the inner skin sheathing the individual cloves may be anywhere from nearly purple to something near the color of photographic paper turning in the sun, a kind of mauvish tan. This type of garlic is often braided into those long spinal-looking ropes that come out of Mexico. From my own experience and that of my customers, there is very little difference in taste between the types of garlic, though the top-setting bulb is remarkably easier to open and peel. It seems almost anxious to slake off its skin, its clothing, and to offer itself up for delectation. As a result many people think it tastes better.

There is a reason for this. The bulbs of your more common non-bolting type generally consist of an outer ring of larger cloves enclosing a cluster of smaller, sliver-like cloves which can be exasperatingly small to grasp and peel, particularly in a small bulb. What the top-setting type does in effect is to transport the plant material of this inner ring way up its hollow stalk, to an elevation of from two to three feet above the ground, and transform it into a pod full of up to a hundred garlic bulblets—or, properly, bulbils—that range in size from a grain of wheat to a grain of corn. In time, the pod unsheathes, drops away, leaving a mauvish berry-like cluster of bulbils exposed to the sun.

Then what? Some biped or quadruped charges through the field or a storm comes up, and the cluster shatters and scatters tiny garlic bulbils over the landscape, in a radius of from three to ten feet. My neighbor's horse, in the course of galloping across a field, could easily propel a seed cluster even farther.

Top-setting garlic, unlike non-bolting commercial cultivars which can only clone themselves from year to year through time and history, can both clone and seed itself—or, more properly, clone itself both below and above ground. Though the top-setting inflorescence bears tiny pink flowers, they're sterile, so the bulbils are not in fact seeds so much as more cloned plant material, yet they enhance the plant's reproductive chances by a factor of ten—or even more when you consider the increased range of the above-ground bulbils.

What follows is an unproven theory. What I would posit is that over the millennia growers have bred out of garlic just this capacity to send up a seed stalk with all those hundreds of bulbils swaying back and forth three feet above the ground. Anybody who farms generally wants garlic to grow only where it is planted, not all over the place. Our collective human wisdom wanted garlic to concentrate on its bulb. We wanted a tight bulb, not a loose, almost fragile one. We wanted one that could store and ship longer, look nicer, even if it was drying up inside its attractive layers of skin while it sat on the hot shelves of Babylon, Nineveh, or Luxor. Like all imperialists, we said: All those seed stalks get in the way, all those tiny bulbils end up infesting our other crops, we have garlic in our wheat and rye fields, and all our bread tastes of garlic, it gets into our orchards and begins flavoring even our fruit. We're going to select against bolting and in favor of non-bolting. It's part of a deal. You give up a pretty good place in the evolutionary rat race and we'll take care of you, we'll make you a domesticated crop, which means as long as we're running the planet you'll be just fine.

All this was before nuclear weapons, acid rain, the destruction of the rain forests, global warming, and those other things that suggest maybe we won't be kept on as managers of the planet much longer.

As a result of our long-range breeding programs to select for non-bolting, not much top-setting garlic is grown commercially in this country. As I said, the stalk gets in the way of cultivation and harvesting and the bulbils will soon infest a field with tiny garlic plants, and the bulbs are not as tight or white as the other kind. Top-setting garlic is, however, easier to peel and the individual cloves are bigger. And as I said, some people think it tastes a lot better. I've had customers over the years tell me it's sweeter, sharper, more pungent, smoother, milder. I'm sure they're all correct, particularly if they're comparing my garlic with the dried up stuff they've been buying from the stores all winter.

By now you've guessed that the garlic I grow is the top-setting type. I may even have the largest planting of it in the United States of America.

My vast plantation of the crop measures about an acre and a half.

＊

6

CROPS, WORDS,
MOVIES

CULTIVATED CROPS, like words, like language, are things that glide into view out of the murkiness of the past. I think of my words as mine, but the chances are that even after fifty or sixty or seventy years of chewing on them, writing them down, word-processing them as a speaker and as a writer, I won't succeed in putting a single new one into circulation. Same with plants, with crops, as a gardener and farmer. I know that there are weeds out there waiting in line to become domesticated, or even redomesticated in the case of crops that have fallen from grace back into being weeds again. You can tell by the way they hang around the garden that they have adapted themselves to our seasonal disturbances, but I doubt I'm the one to figure out what they're good for in relation to the fashions of human existence. What we're given in words and cultivated plants has been worked over for hundreds of generations before it comes to us, and the chances of our adding much to it are very slim. What we add is illusion: each time we're born, the world looks new, is new, which gives us a strange kind of leverage against the weight of accumulated biological and cultural existence, which means for a while, off and on, now and then, under certain circumstances, we believe we are the owners or managers or the franchise operators of this world, not the other way around, and that we have invented almost everything in sight, from the words that drop so easily from our mouths to the plants we grow in our gardens.

It is possible, however, to flip over most of the terms.

I will probably never find out why a particular type of garlic chose me as its husbandman. Using the tools of rationality to figure out how crops, not identifiably articulate or rational in human terms, choose this or that farmer or gardener to grow them will not get you very far. I am reduced to saying things like: I have a certain affinity for this or that plant, and the plant responds to my caring gestures, my tendings, to my delight, my passion, my labor, to my intelligence and intuition attempting to illuminate the universe inhabited by it. There is something very obvious in this. Also something essentially mysterious, at least within a society that has a multivalent attitude toward the simpler forms of biological existence.

Twenty years ago Rose Mary and I moved to a village in a narrow valley of northern New Mexico. We had just seen the film *Easy Rider*. Its message was: Head for the Hills. The hills in question were a southern spur of the Rockies, the Sangre de Cristo Range. Several thousand people did just that. We were among them, a little too old to be hippies, though we tried. The year was 1968, that banner year in American history. Or actually 1969 by the time we got our belongings together and were able to talk our way out of an apartment lease in San Francisco. Conveniently the place had a chronic gas leak.

I don't think there's anything particularly silly about heading for the hills on the basis of a not-especially good film. I went to Greece after seeing *Never on Sunday,* which, when you think about it, is a film about fringe benefits for prostitutes, though the music was lively. I wrote a couple of novels on the islands, and the last of that money was to go to buy our irrigated two-acre bottomland field in northern New Mexico. More important, I met my Australian wife, Rose Mary, on Crete, and she saved me from the perils of a life as an effete expatriate, though gained herself an expatriate's life on a farm in America. A lot of people set off across the prairies in wagons a hundred-and-some years ago on the basis of even less reliable information. Most Native Americans will argue that Columbus should have waited for the movie. And who could have been more deluded than the Conquistadors?

Anyway, that in brief was how we made our way from the island of Crete via Dublin and San Francisco to a lovely little mountain valley in northern New Mexico where we would soon begin making mud bricks for the house we would eventually build with our own hands. And by then we would have two small kids in tow.

Each year, of course, we grew a garden, and each year it got bigger. One spring, 1971 or 1972, a friend brought by a bucketful of plants freshly dug up from an apple orchard a few miles down the road: They were garlic plants. He thought I might like to try them in my vegetable garden. I hadn't had much luck with the bulbs I was buying at the feed store or through mail-order catalogs. I was beginning to think you couldn't grow garlic at sixty-five hundred feet where the winter temperatures had recently dropped to a record-breaking forty below zero Fahrenheit.

One of the things that gardening does for you is to allow you to bring into the world of exchange a wealth of cheap biodegradable goods of unsurpassable quality. All but pathologically stingy gardeners are generous with whatever they grow. This has nothing to do with wealth, the other kind of wealth, which is early schooled against the dangers of generosity. It has to do with natural abundance, with the seeming ease with which plants and trees bear, compared to the onerous labor required to craft anything by hand.

From the point of view of the plant, the bounty is a sur-
vival tactic. We live amid vast seas of the sperm and ova of the
plant world. We help manage the flood, spread it, distribute it,
nurture it, and consume it. Trading seeds and plants is something
we almost instinctively do. We've been doing it for thousands of
years. The plants I grow in my garden and fields originated in
Europe, South America, Africa, Asia, and they were brought here
consciously by human hands. Humankind has been in effect a
force of nature helping distribute plants throughout the planet.
The garlic plants that my friend dug up in his orchard, and which
grow in the wetter spots of countless small orchards in northern
New Mexico, may well be the descendants of plants brought up
from Mexico, brought over from Spain, along with fruit tree
grafting stock, by the same Spanish colonists who were transporting corn, chile, squash, beans, potatoes, and tomatoes in the
opposite direction. My friend moved them only two miles farther
away from their probable place of origin in Central Asia. A journey of ten thousand miles ends with the last step.

It was spring. The plants were young and bulbless, perhaps six inches tall, rather like leeks. I planted them. Neither he
nor I knew that garlic does not like to be transplanted. The results
were not particularly impressive. However I did take notice of the
fact that these vigorous young plants, even though they became
much less so after I planted them, had at least once been thriving
enough to inspire a friend to dig them up and bring them over.
They had still looked good in the bucket.

By midsummer the somewhat sickly plants produced only
small bulbs. But by fall I must have noticed out of the corner of
my eye that the bulbs I missed digging up were sprouting pairs of
rich green leaves. This was an interesting though confusing phe-
nomenon. The various plant encyclopedias I consulted claimed
that garlic should be planted in the spring "as early as the ground
can be worked." The advice seemed to be ill-founded, or else I

was one of those slothful gardeners who did not want to be out in the March winds preparing my garden. Or else the experience of gardeners in radically different climates had been falsely generalized. Or, more likely, one of those inexplicable fissures had opened up between those who farm for a living and thus must know such things, and those who compose idyllic articles for gardening magazines and encyclopedias.

A second messenger arrived bearing a bowl of garlic seed tops, or bulbils, as plucked from garlic growing wild in an apple orchard up the road. I broke up the clusters and planted the bulbils the following spring, a couple of rows a hundred feet long each. I had visions by then of suddenly possessing a lot of garlic. And by then our garden was getting up toward half an acre and we were selling produce in the summer at the farmers' markets in Taos, a thirty-mile drive to the north. The bulbils, the largest the size of a grain of corn, produced a slip of a plant of no more than four leaves that vaguely resembled young wheat or rye and grew no more than a foot high, if that. In July they stopped growing. Then the folded leaves, never very broad in the first place, wilted and died back. I dug up a few plants. They had produced a bulb, but a very small one, rounder than the inverted heart shape of your normal garlic bulb. Further, these tiny bulbs that ran in size from a dime to a quarter had no clove divisions. They were solid garlic flesh. Much later I learned that they were called "rounds."

What to do with rounds? Most of them were too small to sell, too small even to dig up and throw away. Dead end, I thought. I left my couple of rows of rounds in place, neglected them, maybe even tilled under the weeds at one point late in the summer.

In September of most years the Gulf Coast hurricanes shunt masses of warm moist air up over the Sangre de Cristo Range that collide with the drier, cooler air that tends to inhabit the area. The result can be great roiling stacks of thunderheads leading to cloudburst, deluge. The moisture from the fall storms signals the myriad seeds of cool-weather annual and perennial grasses that the time has come to germinate and sprout, root and reclaim the land. It is also a signal to garlic which, as I was about to become aware, shares the same cycle.

The summer-dormant bulbils that had grown into rounds sprouted again in late September. They sprouted just like cloves. They produced a pair of wide folded leaves, lightly tinged with red their first days into the air. The implication was that a grain-sized bulbil, given an extra season in the ground to produce a clove-sized round, would eventually grow into a normal-sized garlic bulb with the usual number of clove divisions. Not surprising, of course, when you come to think of it. That's the sort of thing seeds usually do.

Bulbils also sprouted, but their leaves were as in the spring much finer, thinner, more like those of grasses. Over these couple of years in my haphazard experiments with growing garlic, quite a few bulbs and bulbils and rounds got scattered around the place. In fact I have probably learned as much or more about the life cycle of garlic by observing the behavior of plants that have escaped my control than the ones I have planted. I pretended not to pay a lot of attention to the renegades at first, to the bulbs that got dropped or broken in the shed, raked out into the garden, swept into ditches.

As an educated man it took me many years to figure out a few facts of life, the main one being that the truth did not always announce itself by means of the written word.

The fact of the matter may be that by the time the written words do finally arrive, with all the usual bureaucratic delays, the truth has been sitting around waiting on the edges, in the ditches, by the side of the road, for the longest time.

[29]

＊

7

ONE MAKES TWELVE

WHEN YOU PLANT a clove of garlic in the ground in the fall, nine months later you will get back a bulb of about ten to fifteen cloves. The ratio of what you plant to what you harvest is around one to twelve.

This is very low. Think of a head of wheat or rye, modern strains of which produce a hundred grains for every one sown. One kernel of corn produces a plant that will yield several ears each studded with hundreds of kernels. A tomato plant grown from a single seed can bear dozens of tomatoes each containing scores of seeds. Each pumpkin is a treasure-house of reproductive energy.

Garlic is an exception, at least when it is planted in the conventional manner, by breaking up bulbs into cloves. What this means is that you have to hold back 10 to 12 percent of your crop as planting stock for the next season rather than only 1 or 2 percent or even less. This in turn accounts for the relatively high price of garlic per pound compared to its cousin, the onion, which sets true seeds in abundance.

Over a couple of years I had worked out the life cycle of the bulbil despite an unwillingness to believe in the results of my own experiments. I thought that there's probably a whole college of agriculture somewhere in the country that does little else than study the habits of garlic plants. My faith in the existence of this vast pool of expertise was only slightly shaken by an afternoon spent in the library of the University of California at Riverside, where I uncovered listings of research papers on garlic from the USA, Japan, Korea, the USSR, and France, but no title for the definitive volume on garlic culture that I was convinced must exist. How could it not?

Within a few years of beginning to grow garlic, I had managed to work up a harvest of about 500 pounds a year. If I wished to stay at that, I would have to hold back 50 to 75 pounds to replant in the fall. If I wished to increase production, however, I would have to plant 150 to 200 pounds of my hard-earned harvest, garlic that I was able to sell for a dollar and a half a pound, money I could convert to other kinds of food, to clothing, fuel for my family. I knew of no commercial source from which to buy more top-setting garlic for planting, but assumed—did one exist—that the price would have been in line with what I was selling it for. The top sets or bulbils of my top-setting garlic offered me a way to leap over the usual practice and vastly increase the size of my planting without putting my then entire annual crop of bulbs back into the ground for a year.

About this time we began renting a neighbor's three acres a quarter of a mile up the road. The two fields of that place were good bottomland sandy loam, with the top field of the two containing more clay. It was a lot to take on all at once with my still-primitive equipment, though the fields were still in good shape, having recently been rented by the singing farmer, who had moved his operation to even larger fields elsewhere. I decided to plant the upper field in garlic bulbils.

To plant this half-acre in garlic bulbs broken into cloves, as I was eventually to do, would have taken over a hundred pounds. But only twenty pounds, if that, of the corn-kernel-size bulbils sufficed that spring. I no longer clearly recall my seeding methods, probably because for several months afterward I regarded the whole planting as a failure. The rows came up evenly enough in April, nearly fifty of them, each a hundred and fifty feet long, spaced about two feet apart. Weeds came up too. They grew faster than the tiny garlic slips, which I valiantly tried to weed as long as I could. In early June I simply gave up. I remember having done all this by hand, drafting friends, family, passersby. This was long before we hired anyone to help us at anything. Point of pride here: self-sufficiency meant that you did it all yourself, and alone if possible, because it was good for you.

The field grew high with lamb's-quarters, wild sunflower, and ragweed. Summer passed. The first frosts killed back the weeds and left a tangle of tough, dry hulks. The rains came. Late in September, on one of my inspection walks when I was probably wondering what to do with the half-acre disaster, under the drying stalks of the summer's growth I noticed the even green lines of my fifty rows of garlic coming back to life, files of broad fleshy leaves pushing up through the earth. I tramped my way through and across the tangle. The stand, if I could salvage it, looked excellent. With the action of last spring's attempts at cultivation and now with the tangle of dry weeds, the irrigation furrows were hopelessly clogged; and the field was simply too large to rake clear by hand.

My solution was somewhat primitive and brutal but it worked. Guided by the lines of new growth, I ran the tractor up and down the rows with the furrowing shovels set very shallow. They also served as rakes. They clogged every few feet. I had to climb down, lift the implement, push the piles of dry stalks into the centers of the beds and clear of the irrigation furrows; and later I had to do a lot of hand work deepening the furrows and cleaning them out again. But I was finally able to irrigate the field that autumn, and early the next summer it yielded a harvest of garlic that kicked us well up out of the five-hundred-pound range. Every year thereafter I planted between a quarter- and a half-acre in bulbils for harvest two seasons later, cultivating the field as well as I could until late spring and then letting it go. Until I finally acquired my own tractor-powered mower-mulcher, I hired a neighbor to mow down the weeds at that time of the summer when the ground was dry and when the bulbils, now grown into rounds the size of a dime or a quarter, were safely dormant four or five inches below the surface.

I have since made refinements. My most recent plantings have been with an old John Deere Flexi-Planter, using a corn seed plate to place the bulbils about four inches apart in the row, and using bulbils that have been sized by running them through a seed sizer and cleaner. I now plant the bulbils in October rather than March in order to give them a better start in the spring.

Planting bulbils offers some other advantages. For one, you always have a crop in the ground. There is a kind of security in this. There seems to be no commercial source for top-setting garlic, as I eventually discovered, nothing at all equivalent to the large suppliers of standard non-bolting types in Gilroy whose bulk prices run at about a quarter of retail market prices. In short, in the event of disaster, I would have to replace our crop myself, and it would take me several years starting from scratch. With a half-acre or so of bulbils always in the ground, I could be back in business in a much shorter time.

There is also the obscure matter of human selection for this or that quality in a garlic bulb. When we go through our garlic pile in the shed each summer and fall, we select the nicest-looking bulbs for our arrangements. By all rights we ought to hold those back to replant. All too often what gets chosen by default for planting are the bulbs that don't look very good or are misshapen or somehow odd, whose skins are slaking off—the bulbs that don't get sold at the market. At planting time, at bulb-breaking-up time, I try to correct for this and select some of the best-looking and largest bulbs for planting. But in the frenzy of late summer, with customers buying more garlic than at any other time of the year, sometimes this is difficult. By contrast, selecting bulbils for planting, and they have no other competing use, is more random, and you are also dipping into a larger pool of plant material. I don't sell seed tops, I give them away; and there is no reason not to select the largest bulbils for planting.

Had I enough land I would plant all of my top-setting garlic in this manner. The main disadvantage of the method is that it ties up a field for two seasons for each harvest. This of course might not be a bad thing for the land—or even for the farmer.

✳

8

WATER

I HAVE MENTIONED IRRIGATION.

A reason I got into farming and therefore into growing garlic had something to do with water.

I grew up by the edge of what was called in the family "the stream." It had no official name. Most of the year there wasn't enough water in it to merit the term. Occasionally it flowed, but mostly it trickled, seeped, oozed. The stream ran through a corner of our half-acre property at the bottom of a canyon in an otherwise arid part of Southern California. Its origins were not natural. A half-mile above our place a small reservoir stored water pumped in from the Colorado River or down from the Owens Valley, and our stream was the trickle that seeped out from beneath its rip-rap dam and made its way down the uninhabited canyon, feeding clumps of cattails, sumac, and willow, to a cement culvert under a road that conveyed it into our property, where it flowed into a small pond. My father had made the pond by building a cement wall between two bluish granite boulders. The spillway consisted of dark, algae-grown planks set in an opening in the wall. On one side of the pond he had added a half-sunken cement bench, where you could sit with your feet in the water. On another side he had framed up a potting shed of splintery green lath; when friends of my sister's and mine came to play, it served as a jail in our moralistic games. At the entrance of the pond, near the mouth of the culvert, he had planted a tall variety of bamboo and had built a rickety bridge across the two-foot deep water where, very young, we were sat down to eat lunch out of paper bags, with legs dangling over the scratchy boards, and admonished not to fall into the clear water whose still surface was plied by water spiders.

In summer the stream sometimes dried up and the pond lowered and became too dank to paddle in. And in winter during the sometimes long rains the channel swelled with muddy brown water and overflowed the dam, and the occasional wild duck would ply its way upstream or down. The stream and the pond were my childhood companions, they were a playground, they were books and television, they were the mirrors of a gangly and contemplative Narcissus. In the splashings of any pool there is whatever one will need to see: the dream of everything, the nightmare of nothing, clouds and stars, a self.

I acquired certain tastes in the matter of bodies of water. I shrank from small inland lakes, even high altitude ones, which seemed too lifeless, cold and still. Large ones of the oceanic class, the Lake Michigans, proved surprisingly acceptable. Small streams and ponds of any type, yes, I would pause to investigate their flows and the life that teemed in and around them, while large rivers attracted me from afar but then disappointed me close up. Seas and oceans, because they churned with directionless life and movement, I could sit beside their vast melancholy spaces for lifetime after lifetime were the means provided. Then there were those tiny trickles I would seek out in the brush-covered hills of Southern California that would run for a day or two after a long rain, and cause little mounds of moss to grow in shadowy places.

I spent the first thirty years of my life within sight of the Pacific, then Lake Michigan, then the Seine, then the Aegean, and then the Irish Sea, before I moved a thousand miles inland to New Mexico to a small tributary of the upper reaches of the Rio Grande. In my travels I had passed through Granada and had been enraptured by the little channels and the pools and fountains of the Alhambra, and the ease and inventiveness with which water was moved about in order to comfort and delight, and to mark the hours and days, and to accompany the night, and to feed the eye and the ear and the sense of touch, and to nourish perhaps the dream of the always aquatic return.

Through the backyard of the first house Rose Mary and I rented in New Mexico, an old adobe a mile or so upriver from the two-acre field we were to buy a year later, there flowed a community irrigation ditch, an acequia, one of nine in the narrow mountain valley. When I first walked down through the weed-grown backyard and stood on the plank bridge that crossed its five-foot width, and followed with my eye the leisurely downstream course past the apple tree that grew from its south bank, and watched it flow beneath the barbed wire fence that marked the edge of the property, in some obscure sense I realized I had come back home. In that backyard, on perhaps a twentieth of an acre, with water pumped out of the acequia, we were to grow our first garden.

*

9

THE POUND WEIGHT OF
THE REAL

As ONE WHO grew up in a suburb whose street names were
in a language nobody who lived there actually spoke, and as
one who went to a university whose Gothic buildings were
imitations of others elsewhere, presumably genuine, I
developed a craving for what I called the real. No matter
that such distinctions are the stuff of unending philosophical
dispute. Or that there are occasions, as age will tell you,
when the unreal is much to be preferred.

Also when very young an ambition was placed in my
head. I was six. I was playing with some square ceramic tiles
of the small, smooth variety once used to face kitchen coun-
ters. They were tan. When struck against each other they
made little chinking noises, almost like coins. I was building a
little house. I remember the presence of a tall gray-haired
woman bending over me and saying, "You should be an
architect when you grow up."

There were the other usual misunderstandings. Over
the years these accumulated and led to that climactic moment
on the morning of May 31, 1971, when Rose Mary and I
shoveled some mud out of a wheelbarrow and down into the
roughly nailed-together wooden rectangle that would hold

our first adobe brick. The day was windy and clear but rudely cold. Shoveling the dry dirt into the wheelbarrow, then adding water and mixing it had been an awkward, uncertain business. Were we doing this right? The solitary brick dried in two or three days. As it dried, it cracked. It cracked so badly that to think of building a whole house of such things would be madness. We had done something wrong. With this most elemental of building materials, the earth itself, which everybody in the so-called underdeveloped world, all over the Americas, Africa, and Asia, knew how to use except us—we had failed.

For months beforehand I had carefully read books, interrogated our fellow newcomer Anglos, who were hesitantly building the first rooms of their small houses, and Hispanic neighbors who had built their own adobe houses, or who had helped their fathers and mothers, their aunts and uncles build theirs, or repair or add on to houses built by their grandparents and beyond. I learned from them all that it could be done. But there was still something missing in the how, which had to do with the actual doing of it.

Finally we hired the village outcast to instruct us in brickmaking. Cleofes Quintana (as I will call him) lives behind the village store with a demented sister who for many decades has conducted ritual shopping trips to the store for her wedding accessories. Cleofes travels around town on foot or by hitching rides, and the goal of his activities is to find something to drink. Discourse with him always turns to the moon and to the eating of chile and beans and therefore to gas; were Cleofes capable of sustained rational conversation he would no doubt posit the theory that the test of a good meal is the amount of flatulence it produces, or even that such is the purpose of feeding oneself.

However, Cleofes knew how to make adobe bricks.

He is a round little man with small merry features set in a pumpkin head. He liked to talk as he dug up the rich brown earth and shoveled it into the wheelbarrow and mixed it into mud, and chattered away about the moon, chile, beans, punctuating his words with gleeful sound effects and giggles—while the too-earnest students of his craft noted his gestures and vainly attempted to solicit pointers.

"Cleofes, how do you know when you have enough water?"

"Real good chile, lots of beans," says he, followed by simulated explosions, winks, a humming giggle. "Drink lots of beer."

Thus we learned how to make adobe bricks. I built a form for four adobes in the shape of a ladder, each compartment twelve by eighteen by four inches; this we laid on the dry ground raked smooth and scattered with straw before pouring into it the overflowing contents of the wheelbarrow. It turned out that the dirt from what was to become our front yard was perfect for adobes and required no additives except straw; it dried into a rock-hard brick that required vigorous blows from a hatchet to trim.

To make adobe bricks by hand you have to lift vast amounts of weight countless times. First you have to shovel up into the wheelbarrow the mud which you set to soaking in either a volcano-like pile or else a pit the night before. Then you wheel your laden wheelbarrow, weighing two-hundred-and-some pounds, over to a flat area where you will lay out the bricks. Then you can half-shovel, half-pour the contents down into the form. It takes two people to lift the form free of the wet adobes, which are the consistency of chocolate mousse. At this point the muddy form goes into a fifty-five-gallon drum to soak while the next wheelbarrow-load is mixed. In a day or two you'll tip the bricks up on edge, to speed their drying. In a week or so you'll carry them over to the edge of your work area and arrange them on edge in stacks that lean against each other like books on a shelf and where they will complete their drying. You'll lift them one or two more times when dry: once onto the truck or tractor or wheelbarrow that will carry them over to your building site, and then again to set them into place on the wall you are constructing.

Each of our bricks weighed 55 pounds. On the average we probably lifted each brick five times that summer. You might say that the working weight of each brick was therefore 275 pounds. Add another 20 to 30 pounds per brick for your adobe mortar and interior and exterior adobe plaster. So make it 300 pounds per adobe brick.

The first two rooms of our house, which we built from June to December of 1971, needed fifteen hundred such adobes, which meant the lifting of about a half million pounds of earth in various forms. Each of the rooms was twelve by eighteen inside, with nine-foot ceilings. Add countless truckloads of sand and rock for the foundation, fired brick for the kitchen floor, more mud for the living room floor, plus a truckload of sixteen-foot ponderosa pine logs for the ceiling beams, another truckload of both rough and finished lumber for ceiling planks and door and window frames and lintels; plus many loads of earth for our traditional dirt roof which soon leaked but was—at least—cheap to put on. In all I would estimate that we moved over three hundred tons or some three-quarters of a million pounds of material during about five months. This works down to about two tons a day. Of that I probably moved well over half myself.

Rose Mary and I in fact did little else that summer besides move building material. Two sets of friends, also on food stamps, offered to help us make our adobes, and we soon established a regular morning schedule of two days working and one day off that gave us our fifteen hundred adobes in about a month. Friends and family helped us pour the foundation during a long day in August, and they came again to help us set the vigas and nail down the ceiling planks in October. I had a thirst then for lifting things, for moving them. I was in my mid-thirties. I had spent my adult life first as a student, then as an expatriate writer doing nothing more strenuous than lying on beaches or lugging suitcases from one Aegean watering hole to another. I was intoxicated with my newly discovered physical power. Most of all I loved to drive our old 1947 Chevy one-ton flatbed up into the arroyos to gather stones for the foundation or for the courtyard I would later lay or the stone tower we would build down in the field as my writing studio. The windy, sandy arroyos were like beaches, the rocks and boulders like giant seashells in the glare of the high summer sun, a random churning of granite, shale, quartz, basalt, lignite. For the charcoal brown basalt we would build the tower from, we found a dirt road up to the mesa north of the valley where we picked stones out of the hillside and loaded them onto the truck, in the sage-scented heat. There I also found a rounded, shapely basalt-like stone that had been weathered by the actions of the ancient inland sea that had once washed over the area. I thought it would look nice in our future courtyard. It weighed perhaps 150 pounds. I am six-feet-three. Later I came to call it my hernia stone.

We built through two summers, adding a back room for the children the second year and completing the stone tower down in the orchard. The gasping labor required to hoist the fifty-five-pound adobes from the back of the truck up onto a ten-foot parapet had caused me to scale down the following year's batch to twelve by twelve by four inches weighing about thirty-five pounds each. We took the third season off for our operations, Rose Mary's worsening varicose veins, and my hernia. We resumed the fourth year and added two bedrooms, made out of adobes scaled down yet further to the size of large loaves of bread and weighing seventeen pounds each, bricks small enough for even children to handle. Finishing work, detail work, correcting early errors, will no doubt occupy us the rest of our lives.

So the real had to do with weight, with the labor of one's own hands, and with the earth itself; it is what gives anchor and ballast to all the flighty unreality, the soarings of the mind that guide the hand; and though it bestows a familiar confidence with the material stuff of existence and can deliver moments of piercing joy, it must also, to be what it is, open wounds of pain and fear and despair.

I write these words within walls of earth twelve inches thick and built with the help of friends, from a lesson taught by the wisdom of an idiot.

*

10

WHICH LEADS TO THE
SUBJECT OF VAMPIRES

OVER THE PAST DECADE we've sold perhaps fifty thousand pounds of garlic. We've sold it off the back of the truck at markets. Bunched and braided we've sold it at craft fairs. We sell it at the farm, at our shop in Taos. I would estimate that one out of every five customers makes a remark or asks a question about vampires. One out of a hundred, having made such a remark, will give a shake of the head and turn to me and say, "I'm sorry, you must have heard that a thousand times."

"Yes," I'll say back. "But that's all right."

It's true that I've neglected to interrogate all these people about exactly what they mean by vampires. I haven't asked my customers whether we're talking about blood-sucking bats, nocturnal predators in general, zombies, or what. I suppose this means that I think I know what we're talking about. They also must assume as much.

The vampire my customers and I have silently agreed on is perhaps a kind of media creature, a humanoid bat-like being recently risen from the grave, the sort of creature that will lean over your bed at night and sink its sucker-like fangs into your neck and feed there for a while. As a garlic grower whose front yard is littered with pungent-smelling residue, and as a man who has built his garlic shed just outside his bedroom window and commonly sleeps each night within twenty yards of several tons of garlic bulbs, I am presumably safe from such nocturnal intrusions.

But what about them? What about those thousands of customers who have walked up to the back of my pickup with their vampire remarks—what is troubling them, what is leading them to broach this subject well before introductions are exchanged? In what particular way might these vampires be bothering them?

If pressed my customers would probably brush aside the question. They would pack it away into the category of one of those silly social remarks, just something to say in order to make contact, like talking about the weather. But the weather is conveniently there. It's there outside or overhead or all around to be discussed, analyzed, compared, complained of, celebrated, remembered. There is something deeply functional in talk about the weather: in it we gossip about the planet itself.

The question usually takes a form something like this: "I'll bet you're not bothered by vampires around here." In fact less a question than an assertion with a rhetorical spin that attempts to cut out the problem of the reality or existence of these creatures at the same time. A remark that simultaneously excuses itself for being unimportant. In short, a claim for attention.

Let's rephrase the question. We're at the Farmers' Market on the Sanbusco Center parking lot on Montezuma Street in Santa Fe one Saturday morning. The sun's just beginning to clear the top of the building that houses the movie theater that used to be called the Collective Fantasy, and the brilliant light is fanning out to illuminate the boxes and baskets of fresh fruit and vegetables and flowers that fifty farmers and gardeners are struggling to set up for display before the morning rush begins. The parking lot is charged with a mixture of early-morning ill humor and tight-lipped courtesy as startlingly beautiful shapes are materializing out of the backs of pickups. I'm squeezing backward out between the passenger side of my pickup and the driver side of the one parked in the next space, trying to maneuver a lug box filled with garlic bulbs without scratching the paint of either truck. I swing around and set the wooden box down on.my trapezoidal stand of old planks and apple boxes. You are standing there watching me.

"I'll bet you're not bothered by all the things that I am, are you?" you say. I stare at you. It's five to seven. I have been on the road an hour. I've been up since quarter to five. My grasp on where I am or what I'm doing is sometimes not secure at this hour. Several years ago before I was quite used to the early market hours I once fell asleep brushing my teeth in front of the bathroom mirror.

What can I say? "Yes, as a matter of fact, I sometimes am bothered by all those things." I have no idea of what you are talking about. All I know is that most likely the garlic flat I have just put out will not attract much attention until about half the baskets of flowers have sold, as if garlic is something people find difficult to buy too early in the morning, while the memory of last night's dinner is still in the depths of the throat. Yet you are placing a hand in the garlic box and are beginning to rake through it.

Now I begin to understand. By "all those things" you mean children, taxes, aging parents, neighbors, the boss, the company, the corporation, the institution, the military budget, death, television, driving, flying, shopping, the grinding passage of time—any one of which can suck you dry at a time when you'd rather dream and create. All those things add up to rob you of your vitality. They'll drive you to seek cures and thera-

[46]

pies and credits and degrees or a new spouse or travel or gurus promising enlightenment. Eventually early one Saturday morning you will find yourself standing before a middle-aged man with gray hair and a patient, self-satisfied expression, and who is selling garlic out of the back of a pickup. Unthinking, you'll toss out the seemingly flippant question that conceals a lifetime of hurt and disappointment: "With all this garlic I bet you don't have any trouble with vampires, do you?" And instead of him looking you straight in the eye and delivering the words that will free you at last from your nightmares, from all those who are sucking away the substance of your being, the words that will liberate your spirit into the spangled flux of the universe—instead of this, what is he going to say? He'll give you a quick dismissive glance and twist up his mouth and come out with a puckered up "No" accompanied by a small puff of steam.

"I'll take half a pound," you'll say with all the weariness you can summon up. "I sure hope it keeps."

I'm supposing that the cosmic questions are what are really on my customers' minds. And that the presence of a box full of garlic causes them to discharge in the manner of static electricity: "No vampires around here!" Or that there is something unique or unusual about the fact of a man standing beside a pickup filled with his own produce that makes people think, "Ah, the simple life. And without vampires, too." Standing there with my garlic and onions and flowers spread out on upturned apple boxes and plywood planks, perhaps I present a satisfying illusion of self-sufficiency and individualism, of a man wresting a living from the very earth itself, directly without human intermediary, against a sound track of rushing water and chirping birds and crickets, the plop of ripe fruit plummeting through lush grasses. Presumably I don't have to get up in the morning except when I want to or show up for work in my fields except when I'm in the mood, and can take long naps in the afternoon, go on vacation whenever I want. I'm my own man. I have no boss or supervisor. I'm untrammeled by any labyrinthine organization chart. I don't have to worry about channels or protocol. Nor am I trapped in a treadmill of salary scales, fringe benefits, insurance or retirement schedules; nor do I have to nurse my sick-leave days and vacation time; nor will I ever be laid off, transferred, RIFfed. As I stand there shifting my weight from one foot to another to keep warm and stay awake, trying to fix a pleasant and tolerant grin on my face, I am free of that vast social conspiracy by which so many people trade in their freedom for a good life—or so it might seem to those who walk past my stand and who are visited nightly by the vampires of betrayal, guilt, fear, and disappointment.

Yet I live in the same world as my customers, otherwise we could not talk to each other, otherwise we wouldn't so readily agree what a vampire might be. But I live on the edge of what many of them inhabit the center of. It is true that I am my own man in somewhat larger degree than many, yet my life is no simple life. Growing garlic doesn't free me of the need to shop in supermarkets, or negotiate with insurance companies or the government or school systems or hospitals or weapons makers or the ozone layer or much of anything else; and except in the one fact of how I make my living, as a self-employed farmer and writer, I'm as deeply entangled in the webs of institutionalized inertia as the next person.

My vampires are alive and well, thank you. My customers, however, might rather see me as one who has liberated himself from it all, through the thoughtful choice of the simple life. It would not do to disappoint them in this.

"Ha! I'll bet there are no vampires around your farm."

I look up. Then I glance away.

"No, ma'am. Not a one."

＊

1 1

BURIED BLOSSOMS

IT IS OCTOBER. The garlic is planted. Three hundred
pounds, broken up into cloves, sit in even rows six inches
beneath the surface of the sea of soft earth.

In the slanting afternoon light, shadows pool in the
grooves and creases of the newly worked fields. The raw earth,
recently tilled and furrowed and then shaped and planted, lies
coverless to the lowering sun and the faint sweet breezes of
autumn. Wood smoke is in the air again: piñon, juniper, pine.
The earth, the soil of my small fields, a mousy brown substance when moist, is what I peer down into from my tractor
seat hour after hour in my work of tillage and planting, as I
creep along at a mile an hour or less, as I have year after year;
earth I also cross on foot countless times each year, earth in
which I dig, over which I crouch, on which I kneel, earth I
have raised up around me as the walls of my house.

The finally planted fields resemble embossed pieces of
fabric or paper, in large. There are the herringbone tracks of
the eighteen-inch-wide tires, a yard and a half apart, and
between them the raised and grooved tracks of the canted
packing wheels of the transplanter, twin lines twenty-two and
some inches apart beneath which lie the naked cloves. At

each end of the field there will be the scuffling marks of tractor tires making a tight turn, there will be little eddies of
white garlic skin where my workers will have winnowed
loose skin and dirt and roots from the cloves by raising hand-
fuls into the breeze and letting them drop back into the bins,
there will be the odd clove or two that bounced out or
dropped from the planter as I was lifting it out of the soil. The
fresh imprint of the machinery will hold its crispness a few
days, even a week, or until a wind rises and blurs the sharp
edges, or until it rains or snows, or until the neighbors' dogs,
always excited by a freshly worked field, slip through the
fence to play in the dirt at dawn and impress their tracks and
the marks of their rollings over those of my machinery. On
my walks for a few days after planting I will admire my own
handiwork, this embossing I have made on the face of the
earth, or will fret over those rows I have inadvertently put a
wiggle in, the ones that are less than perfectly straight and
which will come to exasperate me in the spring during the
first cultivations. Yet I am pleased that I can now read these
surfaces at a glance. Only a few years ago it was all a mystery
to me, even what was directly under my nose day after day.
There is a kind of knowledge that can be obtained only by a
long succession of small or even absentminded observations
and which remains so private that you fail to see it for what it
is, and so entangled is it in a habitual activity spread out over
many years. And to whom would you speak of the inner life
of your fields?

The garlic is planted, safe in the ground. Even horses
and cows can walk across the field and not damage it. I will
be annoyed at them or their owners only because of the way
the animals' oblique and heavy ploddings deface my own
more delicate markings: otherwise they do no harm to the
deeply planted cloves.

After garlic-planting time, the summer's other crops can be tilled under. From my tractor seat, foam plugs stuffed into my ears, cap shadowing my face, wristwatch dangling from a knob, I watch the withered residues of summer disappear beneath me. The rows of brown and shriveled squash vines go under, and those of their fruit we left behind on the last picking because they were too small or were damaged or misshapen. Sliced in half or half-submerged, bright orange acorn squash come to sit on the smooth brown expanse of freshly tilled earth like floats or buoys. Then the statice flowers, whose stalks emerge from a tight crown and a compact mass of roots, and which the rototiller will often snag and fling about without chopping up. Two passes, the second in third or fourth gear, will often be needed to chop them into smaller pieces. And then the rows of strawberry popcorn on the rocky ground across the river. Then the vegetable garden in front of the house. Then the onion and leek patch, last to be harvested.

I always fret and mourn in this work, though with time I pay less attention to these mewlings. That the squash crop didn't yield as much as it might have because I didn't manure it well enough. Or though the statice bloomed far beyond my expectations we still lost too much to blossoms falling over in the mud and bending into unmarketable shapes. It is always a little sad to see a field go under. Would there have been a last gleaning worth the time and the delay? The days rapidly shorten and grow cool, and an early snow can endanger a fall planting schedule. And though the statice plants will look remarkably healthy despite the nightly frosts of October, I know there isn't enough heat or light in the day to bring the abundant buds into bloom. The plants are not native to this foothill valley of sixty-five hundred feet, and their dark green foliage stands out in a landscape going into tans and yellows and oranges. Cottonwoods, gray trunks curving over the fields from the edges, drop their leaves like schools of golden fish. The flowers' time is up. They must make way for winter wheat or the last garlic planting. The sixteen whirling L-shaped tines of hardened steel shred and bury half-open sprays of purple and light blue and pink and yellow and white, in swaths forty inches wide.

Reason as I will, I am slightly ashamed.

✳

1 2

DECEMBER LIGHT

THERE ARE THE LAST chores of the season: cover the garlic
and onions and squash with old blankets and sleeping bags
and tarps in the shed; straighten up the two sheds; change
the oil and grease the tractor and trucks, hose them down
and wax them; clean up the yard; stack the firewood.

Then I walk. I take two or three walks a day during
the winter, pacing up and down the dirt road from our place
nearly up to the highway, a half-mile east, and then back
down past our gate to the end of the road at the Valdez cattle
guard, and then back again, often with a short excursion over
to the river, to the skimpy rock-tossed beach where we lie
each afternoon in summer. There will be crusts of ice along
the edge. Sometimes a pair of mallards will rise noisily from
the water. The stream never freezes solid along here, and you
can measure in a rough way the weather in the mountains by
how much water is flowing past.

Sometimes, when the ground is frozen or dry, I'll
walk up through the Richardson field, which we rent, or on a
warm afternoon Rose Mary and I will scramble up the steep
and gravelly slope behind the house to the north, and will
climb to the top of the mesa that overlooks the long narrow

valley and where stunted bonsai-like piñon and juniper trees grow. Panting, we will sit down on a rock amid small islands of grama grass clinging to life in the gravel, and we'll look down on our lives spread out in small far below, and on all those that adjoin ours, and on the sweeping reddish hills that embrace what in the warmer seasons is such a narrow little fold of fertility. It is easy to fall into the habit of thinking that winter is a gray, dull time, and pained by the cold and dryness to turn your back on the haunting beauty of northern New Mexico in the low winter light, with its long brilliant shadows. It is perhaps the sharpness of everything being transformed into light without warmth that tricks the mind, and the sense of touch withdrawing into a dry shell like a snail, and of sound become sharp and piercing, too raw. The days shorten. Indoors, turning page after page of whiteness and blackness, you will feel bereft of the sensuous richness of summer and autumn, and the world will come to seem as if it has gone to memory.

Until again you reacquire a taste for the ripening winter landscape, for the light and smoky grays of tree trunks, the black traceries of intertwined branches against a brilliant blue sky, the reds of clays and grays and blues of gravel on the surrounding cliffs and hillsides; the umbers of fallen, curling leaves, the dry grasses; the textures and glints of rocks in the low inspecting beam of the sun in midafternoon on a south-facing hillside, where there can be warmth even in the depths of January. There is an encyclopedia to be composed on the patterns of snow melting, those shards of cloud fallen to the ground beneath a tree or behind a clump of grass or in the furrows of a field, over the course of weeks of slowly rising sun after the winter solstice; of icicles forming and dissolving in the exposed roots of a bank cut away by the flow of the river; or of the months-long collapse of the stalks of weeds and grasses.

Until you finally embrace the cold again and hunger for its proddings—and grow almost contemptuous of those days of thawing and their enervating warmth, and you worry that winter will soon be over. Winter is a time of promise because there is so little to do—or because you can now and then permit yourself the luxury of thinking so. You can wait the days through, the soft windless afternoons briefly warmed and illuminated by the low sun, through December, January, and even February. Later, in March, time begins to run short, all is hurried by the wind, and soon the dreams of winter will give way to the simpler need for rest for the body and to the more practical necessity of making plans for the next day, which will be busier and more demanding; and you will be left with a longing for the simplifications of winter—when you need only imagine spring, not live it, not endure it.

My pacings, sometimes morning, almost always noon and then again at dusk, along a dirt lane lined with cottonwood and New Mexico olive and squawberry and juniper, measure out my most habitual universe and compose the physical dimensions of that which is most real to me: a long adobe house at the north end of our two-acre strip of land, up against the hillside, which presides over a couple of patches of lawn and a half-dozen apple trees beneath which I park most of my farm implements, angular shapes of steel painted yellow and green and red emerging out of the snow; the winter ruins of the vegetable garden; a small round pillbox of a building made of stone, which we call the tower; and the garlic field, less than an acre here, the smaller of several; the whole bordered by drooping barbed-wire fences overgrown with willow, plum, ash, lilac, and creeper. And as I walk down to the gate and turn left, east, into the road, with the river rustling almost out of sight to the right, south, I pass first my neighbor's neat but intrusive mobile home, which was towed in a couple of years before to occupy a neglected apple orchard. The dogs run inside the fence along here and then dart over to the river side of the road, sniffing out the most recent map of what has passed through in the night. Another mobile home set well back from the lane to the left, the Atencio place, with a prosperous woodpile next to the garage, then a couple of overgrown fields, and then the Arellano house nearly hidden behind leafless apple trees; and then the Richardson place, house tucked away behind the bare branches of apple, pear, and cherry trees, above the ditch, with the field stepping down and spreading out with the semblance of a delta toward a border of cottonwood and juniper that lines the road. At the slight rise of the culvert through which passes the narrow channel of the Acequia de Apodaca, I pause and reverse my steps.

In a sense I have lived here too long. Too long for an era that celebrates mobility and the rolling stone that gathers no moss—that celebrates the lifelessness of the stone, not what is alive and living. I know too much. I know my neighbors too well, their strengths and weaknesses, their generosities and meannesses. In a small place you come eventually to be almost related to everybody, you become part of the family. In the winter when I would be reclusive, most encounters are painful, even the casual ones on the lane as I walk, even the begrudging waves to those who drive by—anything that causes me to stop my train of thought and to put on the social mask, or to consider how my words will echo within the being of another and thus resonate throughout this small valley where I live. The very trees and hills, and the river itself, are witnesses to much of my life here, to my small triumphs and achievements, as well as to my mistakes and misdemeanors; to that which I love and hate, as well as that which I neglect and remain ignorant of; to what I waste in my life, and in others'. What I know within myself, these fields and mesas mirror in reproach or mockery or celebration or mourning, or more ordinarily in the long waiting that seems in life to be much of what happens, in which nothing happens; and these are the untiring adversaries to all that I would dispute or pester with thoughts of change. My garlic lies beneath the ground in neat, even rows, and while it is there I too live a kind of subterranean life—indoors, in abstraction, in books, in pieces of paper and notebooks, making my way across those small white fields with meticulously applied marks. Farming and writing are both labors, I once suggested to a friend, that are conducted on flat planes and in relative solitude. It is here in the Pascalian room, which embraces not only the room in which I write but also the landscapes out the window I regularly prowl, that I am most free to reconstruct the world on more acceptable lines, to imagine others, or the destruction of this one, as removed as I choose to be from the emanations of the metropolis. Each time I buy a newspaper or reach to turn on the radio or open a magazine, I make a conscious decision to keep up with the mechanical rabbit of official cultural life; and each time I refrain, or refuse, and leave the paper at the store, and the radio silent during dinnertime, and the television eye dormant through the night, I make another kind of decision, for another kind of center to a life. The bounds to my imagination are no further than the words of the woman with whom I live or of my grown children on their visits back home, or the remarks of the village postmaster, the proprietor of the local store, or the village outcast sputtering of the moon and beer: which is to say that I will heed them to one degree or another, depending on the tenacity of my own ideas and imaginings; and at times they will tell me I have not heard them at all.

Yet the great danger of living in a small place, in rela-

tive solitude, in an almost resistanceless state, lies in formulat-
ing generalizations that will readily crumble elsewhere. For
this reason I will take the occasional long drive to the West
Coast or to another state. Train trips and flights will serve as
well, though your passivity as a passenger can lead you into
the delusion that the world is an easeful, effortless place. No
precise questions are answered by these trips. I am only
reminded that this is an enormously wealthy and varied
nation, yet also an insensitive and cruel and deadening one,
and that to strive for recognition or wealth within it is a dis-
quieting, unceasing labor that will not bring the best out of
any man or woman. Better perhaps to seek the contentment
of more humble work within the belly of the beast, to inhabit
the Pascalian room, to chop your wood, haul your water;
better perhaps to stay at home and grow your patch of garlic,
and to dream in winter your subterranean dreams, which are
always the same: of light, of warmth, and of liberation.

*

II

WINTER:

BORDERS

✳

13

WAITING

ONE OF THE SINGULAR characteristics of garlic is that it makes you wait.

For radishes and spinach, you need to wait only a month or so. For lettuce or carrots or summer squash or green beans you can begin to taste the results of your plantings in two months. Tomatoes and eggplant and peppers and winter squash need another month. But for garlic you must wait seven to nine months from the time you plant to the time you harvest, and during perhaps half of the growing cycle there's little to look at besides a few shoots sticking up here and there in a row. A radish seed will be up in a few days. A garlic clove planted in September in the north may not bother to send up any leaves until March or even early April.

A sense of waiting may have to do with the fact that we are two things at once: creatures of nature, yet creatures estranged from nature. In waiting, we grope along a border that lies both within us and without. I took up farming in part because I wished to explore that distance and that border. I wished to be in contact with the earth, the sky, with water, with plants and animals. Not only that, but in some working relation in which a sense of intellectual detachment would have to yield. I didn't figure this out ahead of time. The thought comes only later, on reflection, and in particular out of those long months of waiting that garlic, more than any other vegetable crop, imposes on you.

To grow garlic means that you have to put your attention to something else much of the time. It follows that you ought not to grow garlic unless you are willing to let it make you as patient as it needs for its purposes.

Waiting or the stillness of some kinds of waiting, the immobility, the forms of waiting that differ from the human-induced wait in that you don't ever quite know what you're waiting for: these are the relaxed and expectant positions in which you can best know the workings of nature. Of course you are waiting for your garlic to come up. But for months there is little to see. So you measure the passage of time against the growth of certain grasses, the patterns of melting snow, the flights of birds, an angle of light, the wind, until gradually you have pulled these things inside you, and one of the barriers has momentarily dissolved, and the distance has been traversed.

See garlic as a pretext for waiting. It has no other way but the long wash of time to extract the sulfur compounds from the soil and to distill them into its distinctive potion: all garlic questions ultimately may have to do with the passage of time, and therefore with mortality, and therefore with vampires, whatever they may be. Hence (if you accept the leaps) the often extravagant claims for garlic's curative powers.

And the time of its hibernation, during which it positions itself to begin gathering its strength, is also a time of our exile. The earth must rest, and there is a sweetness in this, in the pause before the active turn of the cycle, yet also the sadness of all winters. For three long months I am cut off from what I first learned to play in, that in which I dig, tractor on, pat into mud bricks, guide water into, and plant.

Wait. But not kill time. I can savor its subtly wearing passage through me—whatever it is, however it passes through me, like water over a stone, or as through a dog dozing and sniffing the wind—on those sunny and almost warm afternoons when I'll sit out in my father's splintery old captain's chair, in front of the garlic shed, or outside in front of the heat-drinking adobe wall of the living room which is riddled to a shallow depth with holes of some kind of excavating bee; with the dogs lying, muzzles on paws, with the geese picking at the brown lawn and trumpeting their contentment at being out of their pen for the afternoon, while the low sun warms my eyelids and ungloved hands, some quiet afternoon in December or January or February.

The geese are waiting, I know. Their waiting is a sign that they have fallen into the nets and wire fences of human acculturation. They long ago should have left for warmer climates, following the lead of high-crying sandhill cranes that we used to hear on our autumn wood runs, but their own complacency has conspired to keep them here fat and flightless, more or less good-humored, dependent on human needs and uses, one of which is to enliven my winter landscape— and now and then, come spring, to trim the lawn with their nibblings and do a little weeding in the garlic field. They know about waiting. In the winter their feet get cold just like ours. You can tell on those mornings when they're reluctant to lift their down comforters and get up and walk around on the ice.

I will dream there's nothing to do except study the passing minutes and those things that differentiate the instants: jet threading a track high overhead, squawking query of a magpie on a fencepost, whish of the occasional car along the highway a half-mile across the valley, sound less screened now by the bare gray branches of the tall cottonwoods along the river.

My presence slowly slips into becoming ceremonial. I become a ruminating observer of things and poker and prodder of objects during those long stretches of quiet warm weather that frequently becalm our winters. I will stand beside the bright orange tractor with my hands behind my back, like a spectator at a display of agricultural equipment, admiring the lines, the finish, figuring out the clever new features—or pondering the minor repairs and improvements (a rear spotlight to be installed, a tire to be properly patched) that need to be made in the spring, which is still comfortably far ahead. Afternoons are short, too short to do anything, I mutter to myself, so go have a look at the fields if you want something to do—thus urging myself away from that multi-dimensional form of thinking, purpose-oriented, that engages the coordination of hand, eye, mind, and thing: let abstraction thrive.

During the thaws of late January or early February, when the snow cover retreats to the shadows of hedgerows and into the depths of ditches and the dense skirts of juniper trees, I will tramp my fields in search of the first signs of life in the days that are said to be lengthening—although there seems something improbable in the claim: I know I will find nothing more than hints so slight I will have forgotten them by the time I walk back home. A blade of grass a little greener than most in the shelter of the willows, a hint of greenness in the depths of brown tussocks of orchard and timothy grass or at the heart of a scraggly clump of alfalfa. And in fact, as I circle the edges of the fields, earth here still frozen, there now muddy and gummy and too tender to tread on, it may well be in my prowlings and wanderings, in the way I pause and look down a winter-weathered row, that it is my observing presence which is the first and most dramatic sign of the imminent end of the waitings of winter, and that these heavy footfalls on the verges of the fields are, in some sense, also observed.

There is nothing dead about these fields. The weather has been working them hard. The newly thawed and drying earth will be wrinkled and cracked from the daily kneading of freezing and thawing in the nights which can still touch zero degrees Fahrenheit just before dawn, fields which also may have known anywhere from a week to ten nights of the thermometer running down to ten and twenty below. Into the cracks of the frost-fractured surface will be blown the siftings of the sky, which will soon become restless again, filterings of ash and seeds of weeds, particles and grains and chaff, to be buried by the twice-daily shiftings of the soft and powdery soil whose freezings and thawings will have unpacked and fluffed up the trampings and drivings of the previous season. A crust will form and break apart each day, or almost every day, or every day that the sun shines brightly for a few hours in the afternoon, which is most. Forty to a hundred nights of freezing and thawing, fluffing and settling, from mid-November or early December to the first weeks of March: the soil is worked more often and more deeply than my warm weather tractorings, and no doubt to far more beneficial effect: winter renders the soil youthful again.

So I wait for it to do its work. Wait and watch. The days will grow longer. They always have. Those garlic cloves that sprouted and sent up two or four leaves in the autumn will have shriveled back to a washed-out, brown-tinged blue-green, prostrate like withered starfish, easily taken for dead, but they will still be there as the evaporating snows creep back away into the lines of the still-long shadows cast by trees and hedgerows. No new growth will show until the end of February, when the first light green peepings of new leaves will appear.

Dig down—that first thawing day, in the sunniest patch of the field—below the surface, below the still-faintly discernible crease marks left by the packing wheels of the planter. You will find the clove filled out from its tangerine-slice shape to the size and shape of a large olive, with a mass of translucent roots anchoring it firmly to the soil. By now the clove has probably more or less righted itself. And from its top end a whitish knife blade of a leaf will be sprouting, or more properly, twinned leaves acting as one blade, to drive upward through the possibly hard crust. Upon breaking through, which will happen anytime from the end of February until well into April, the leaves will turn to a light green edged with red, as if dipped in a wash, until the eyes of their cells, as it were, adapt to the bright light and begin the work of photosynthesis. Then, as all the leaves emerge fully in late March or April, the green will darken and assume the bluish cast of leeks, whose flat folded form they more nearly resemble than onion plants with their tubular leaves, and whose coloration they will hold until almost harvesttime.

I cannot account for the laggards—those cloves that wait until well into April to start growing, except to suggest that perhaps their winter has been a hard one, they are not well, have been nursing some wound or infection through the cold days and nights, are not certain to live—but in the end, thanks to the antibiotic properties of their own flesh, make a last-minute recovery just in time to catch up with their fellows.

Waiting to heal, waiting to plan. There is something about the unmitigated purity and coldness of the parakeet blue skies of January and February that will finally make the

[66]

mind recoil from its abstractions and seek some warmer, more enclosed space, and move back inside, and welcome back the chores and tasks. I will look at the bare whitish branches of the cottonwood trees, the ones that stand at the edges of my fields, and peer down on the earth I will soon be working again, and I'll think of the trees' long orange roots snaking their way a foot or so below the surface, deep into what I regard as my territories, in order to harvest a bounty of nutrients I have placed there for my more ephemeral plantings. I am only on fair terms with them. I regard them as unkempt and clumsy trees prone to falling abruptly over or dropping their branches at a new twist in the wind, not quite to be trusted either above ground or below. And one of the first tasks I will imagine myself doing in late winter or early spring, as soon as the earth is thawed, is to girdle the borders of my field with a narrow chisel plow set some eighteen inches deep. As I troll the depths the plow's single point will drag some of the roots to the surface. They are like the stems of a giant seaweed plant, or the limbs of some other creature you are not used to seeing on the surface. Here and there the steel will ride noisily over a deep boulder, one that may never work its way to the surface, may even lie there beyond the reach of my normal tillage for the rest of my lifetime.

The earth: that dense, dark sea. When I was a kid, before I knew that such acts might have consequences, I loved to watch the lone bulldozer that carved up the steep hillsides of dark green brush above my house, to know what was beneath those boulder-strewn Southern California surfaces I roamed every afternoon. After school I climbed the hills to watch the big yellow machine carve out shelves for future luxury homes and expose the grainy, orange earth and yet more granite boulders stained orange by the clay. Even today, forty years later, the squeak and clank of their tracks and the roar of those diesel engines sing in my memory as music, not as the cry of devastation. I have long since parted with the steel shoes, the worn dragon's teeth of the ripper blades I used to scour construction sites in search of and with which I built in miniature my own roads and excavated my own sites for houses and cities in a pile of sand or in the bare ground beneath a Valencia orange and a grapefruit tree, at the base of a dripping faucet, with the dismembered branches of a Christmas tree serving to line the streets with evergreen.

The sight of mines, tailing piles, slashing cuts through mountainsides for railway lines, highway excavations, and the visions they conjured up of the earth being torn apart, were scenes I took in breathlessly from the rear seat of a succession of Ford sedans, '32, '39, '49, on our family camping trips through the West before and after the war. Nothing could excite me as much as a vast railway yard filled with hundreds of boxcars and billowings of steam and smoke and the musical roar of shunting diesel-electric engines; and the one thing I long thought myself deprived of as a child was the fact that I didn't grow up next to some magnificent industrial site but instead in an inland suburb, worked over, and only now and then, by a solitary bulldozer operated by a man with a red face.

To wait. To heal. To dream your plantings, to plan to cut those other roots, to accumulate your pungent reserves of sulfur. Because to plant and dream is also to map and explore everything else that would take possession of your fields, and to test your strategies and defenses: in this lies the supreme utility of the dreamer's idleness, and in the cold that arrests almost all but this.

I school myself in waiting. Winter will pass. I pace up and down the dirt road and in and out of the gates to my fields in the low bright sun, and along the stream, which never freezes completely. On the coldest mornings just before the sun fingers its way into the open channel between files of cottonwoods, columns of mist rise above the river, generated by the warmth of the river's flow in contact with the sub-zero air flowing unseen with it, above it, down from the mountains to the east, a respiration that serves as a reminder of the fine edge upon which we live, between the infinite cold that presses down on us from outer space, and the warmth that lies not far beneath our feet, even in the dead of winter.

＊

1 4

A HOPE IN VULTURES

SOMETIMES IT WILL rise just at the moment when a clear
and bright morning becomes warm enough to do outside
work, when you think that winter is ending, when you
have rashly forgotten about the possibility of wind—that
other form of waiting, all noise and rush, theatrical, leading
to nothing more than a suspect stillness. It will blow until
nightfall, a gusting westerly gale that piles tumbleweeds up
against fences and strips wind devils off dirt roads and driveways and scatters seeds from atop brittle stalks of wild sunflower, lamb's-quarters, milkweed, and the tall grasses. The
wind sows, the wind buries, the wind silts up the fine
cracks in the soil which have been opened up by the freezings and thawings of January and February. It finishes the
winter's work and begins the spring's. In northern New
Mexico it rises in March. It can blow into May.

I can eventually acquire a taste for it, for the substance
it can give the day, or illusion of eventfulness, plus a kind of
discipline or direction—once I learn how to keep my hat on
again and to dress warmly enough and to plan my motions a
little in advance, to ignore those pressing and slapping hands,
but yet be willing to retreat in the face of unusual force or

fickleness. A day spent out in the wind is one fully lived even when you are unable to recount coherently a single event—and even as the wind still blows and whirls in memory and imagination. Somehow the wind must serve. How can it not? By exercising the newly emerging garlic leaves it would help right the upside-down cloves. So I reason, at least. Such a grand sweeping force to effect such small alterations. And blow off hats. Or the roof of the shed next door, which I once witnessed out the living room window.

Sometimes I find it better to plunge out into the wind and cold than stay inside and wander from window to window, wondering when it will drop. For the dogs the wind must be a feast of smells rushing through nostrils, a kind of olfactory dream time: perhaps they love the wind, though it may make them less acutely aware of events in space and of spatial relationships in general, and must render fluid what in quiet weather is far more anchored and solid—or if not solid, more nearly plume-like. So a walk in the wind must be a mixture of the familiar, hidden away in the depths of dried leaves and grasses, and of the new and remote sweeping over and through it. In the wind, dogs will orient themselves more visually and will run less in that manic blind way that windless days can often inspire in them.

The wind accompanies those fast-moving storms of late winter and early spring that often seem in too much of a hurry to drop much snow or rain—March, April, sometimes May. On the same currents turkey vultures will soar in from the south, often dropping out of snowstorms to find a traditional perch atop a high dead cottonwood along the river, near the lower end of one of my fields. They will home in, two and three at a time, over a period of a week, until the flock of forty-some has reassembled. They seem soundless, voiceless. I have heard only the whisper of feathers as they take off from the bone-like rocks of the riverbed, surprised by the face of a man peering down at them from the top of the riverbank.

They are part of the circling sky scene over my garlic fields, what I gaze up at and search out in my comings and goings on foot and on my tractor. Once moved back into the valley, the huge birds will drop one by one from their perches into the first dawn breezes and flap their wings until they have cleared the treetops along the river and are settled into a current, then will spiral their way higher and higher into the morning skies, wider and wider, until they disappear over the crests of the hills and cliffs that enclose our narrow valley. Still mornings following upon nights of rain or snow will force them to hang out their long black wings to dry in the sun while they await the first breezes: then the creatures will have to labor their wings up into more active air above the inversion layer settled over the valley.

I cannot quite say what I learn from them or acquire from them, other than the occasional feather; nor is it necessary that there be any more connection than this, the bending over and picking up, a kind of scavenging, of the long black form whose lack of iridescence will distinguish it from the wider tail feather of the magpie. I will take it home and wind it with a bit of twine and hang it up above my desk with others I have found on my walks. In flight they are—or can be—beautiful creatures. Winds arriving late in a day, in April or following a summer storm, while the vultures are circling closer and closer to their roost and readying themselves to drop, with darkness itself, into their dead trees at the very last moment of light. They will pass the last minutes of daylight in playful low-level swoopings, and will weave back and forth over fields and rooftops, and skim the edge of the red clay bluff north of the house and the tops of the cottonwoods that define the lower limit of their flying space.

[72]

I regard them as the elder spirits of the valley. Their seasonal migrations surely predate any human occupation. As a species they have come to know the spring and fall storms well enough to depend on them for their long-distance flights to Mexico, to the Tropic of Cancer, and back; and because they come and go each year without fail, they assure me that the weather we always worry about will remain the same, or enough the same, for things to go on.

When you are close up, when you can make out the red skin of their bald heads, and the whitish tearing beaks, you will know again the instinctual sense of revulsion—yet, finally, at what? We suppose moral superiority because we are able to hire others to kill animals that we may cook the meat: by inference we judge vultures at the visceral level for eating meat that is inelegantly dead by causes other than their own. They are not fellow hunters, not raptors, which we idolize, not thieves of life, but mere thieves of death.

A neighbor chose to be disturbed by them one year. They were roosting in the woods at the bottom of his field. "I don't know what those animals are doing down there," he confided to me one day. I tried to suggest they were harmless, were only resting and sleeping. But true, there is something jarring about the first sign of spring being the arrival of these undertaker birds—in anticipation of the usual disasters, of life struggling out of the ground, out of the shell, out of the nest, of rising waters, sudden cold snaps. Not long ago I rescued a newly hatched gosling from the coils of a king snake, and the memory of carrying the wrestling snake in gloved hands far from the nest, of cupping the warm green gosling weakened by the first encounter of its life and carrying it into the house, will always remain an emblem of the hope and catastrophe of spring. I tried to reassure my vulture-fearing neighbor, but later he must have taken to doing something to chase the birds away, probably in the morning—shouting, pounding on tree trunks, whatever—because they soon moved down the river to a quieter spot, though they will still now and then home in on their old treetop roosts on returning from Mexico.

Like a giant bellows the fickle March winds will also draw migratory songbirds up through the valley toward the mountains when the weather warms, or pump them back down into our sheltered hollows when the snow falls again. Bluebirds, shy apparitions on fenceposts, will flit through on their way east to the high altitudes and then return when mountain conditions become too harsh; then the robins will move back in to ply the lawns and fields, and some will stay and nest. Later in the spring, sharp and plaintive cries down by the river will signal that the killdeer are back scouting the sands for future nesting sites. Barn and cliff swallows wait until the days are warm enough for an abundance of insect life to rise from the earth, and with them come the shy tanagers that work the hedgerows, and the yellow chats that station themselves for a season of singing in the highest treetops. Last of all return the nighthawks, who several stories above the bats will sieve the higher atmosphere of its fine spray of insect protein, an airborne plankton tumbled up from the ground by slow breakers of cool air rolling down each evening from the higher mountains.

Wind-borne seasonal clocks, I suppose—for myself and for the other year-round residents, native and immigrant. The English sparrow, so ever-present as to be almost invisible. The flicker with its coral-pink undersides of wings, whose territory is the ground and tree trunks and the tops of posts and poles, neither quite woodpecker or dove, easy victim of house cats. Birds for whom the spring winds must be as fretful and distracting as for the rest of us who choose to stay in one place while everything else is whipped around by the wind, above the imperturbable ground.

✳

15

MAGPIES

MAGPIES, WHICH I HAVE not mentioned, flirt with the border
from the other side, the side we call nature, the side we think
so veiled from us—because we have set our clocks to run so
much faster and because we so much love flash and noise.

I find myself surprised when a city visitor asks about
"some black-and-white bird" seen down by the road or the
river. Magpies: I thought everybody knew about magpies. I
thought every household within their habitat must have a
flock of dependent magpies by now.

In traditional fashion our adobe living room and
kitchen feature the ends of vigas, the ceiling logs, protruding a
foot and a half through the walls, sticking outside into the air.
After twenty years of exposure to the weather, a few have
rotted off. On the remaining ones the sound of a magpie
alighting during an early morning inspection tour is transmit-
ted right into the house as a resonant scratching—whose
meaning is that the bird is checking to see if we have put the
dog food out the front door yet. If we have, there will be a
second series of sounds an instant later, that of the bird alighting on the rim of the plastic bowl and picking up a lump of
dog food in its beak, followed by another scratching sound as

it jumps aloft and pumps out of sight on beating black-and-white wings. Irritated by these thefts, the dogs will occasionally lie in the shadow of a nearby shrub—a dogwood, oddly enough, a red-twigged dogwood—and lunge out at them.

But the magpies know: dogs are too slow. Cats are not, but magpies, somewhat social creatures, warn each other of the presence of a prowling cat, likely never to reach one of their large twig nests out of embarrassment at the commotion it sets off in beginning to scale or even approach the wild cherry tree in the backyard up on the ditch bank, or the apple tree next to the stone tower, or the cottonwood down by the gate. The birds' jabbering squawks can carry a quarter of a mile on a still day.

Some ten pair forage over the same strip of narrow valley that I do. This works out to about one magpie per cat and dog or one pair per household. Besides magpies I have regular dealings with lizards, toads, frogs, three kinds of snake, mice, gophers, squirrels, two kinds of rabbit, skunks, muskrats, beavers, and perhaps a dozen or more species of birds, plus rare encounters with foxes, bobcats, coyotes, owls, and hawks. Feral pigeons will dig up grain and sweet corn seed and steal feed from the geese, grosbeaks will eat peas from the pod and work at the peaches and plums, crows will devastate a field of corn when flocks of chattering piñon jays don't get to it first—though in the case of sweet corn they are all second in line after the skunks—and scrub jays will systematically extract any corn from dry cobs left uncovered in the shed and will also raid the cats' and dogs' dishes if the coast is clear. Sparrows discreetly work the ground for scraps of all this, then move into the shed in winter where they nibble at the chile strings hanging from the rafters through the long cold nights.

But the most ever-present are magpies, and the most

interested in what I do, in largely a non-predatory way—
outside of matters of dog food. They are carnivores by preference. Dog food will serve, as will grain or old grapes dried
on the vine, but they seem to prefer their meat fresh from
the earth. In my spring tilling and cultivation, two or three
magpies will stride behind the tractor looking for worms and
grubs like seagulls or pelicans following a fishing boat at sea.
They note how rarely I get down from the noisy machine
and how ponderously I do so. They have learned to work
within five and six feet of the whirling steel tines, close to
what for them must be a ferocious din. Gullets full, they fly
off in an oblique line across the field toward a large stick
nest high up in a cottonwood along the river.

I spend a lot of time in their company. But like my
city visitor I once may not have paid much attention to them.
They were there—out there, across that border, somewhere in
nature, a black-and-white bird. Perhaps fifteen years ago a
startling if trivial event finally brought them into focus. My
father and I had just finished setting out two rows of cabbage
plants. We had opened the ditch gate, and the muddy water
was feeling its way down the rows, twin snakes with heads of
white foam. We were leaning on our shovels, resting, basking
in the morning sun, waiting for the water to reach the far end
of the rows. Two white cabbage moths fluttered into view and
converged on the plants, as if in prior knowledge of our
schedule. Then two magpies dropped from the sky with a flash
of black-and-white wing, each taking a row, each patrolling
the slow-moving tongue in search of insects flushed from the
earth by the advancing water. The white of the foam—of the
wings of the moths—of the magpies' markings: were those the
common signals? Was it the uncanny symmetry?

The moment passed. Moths, birds, father and son with
shovels: all went their separate random ways. There is nothing

more. Except the intimation out of the corner of the eye that these things, such symmetries, such patterns, assemble themselves and break apart all the time, everywhere, within the reach of eye and hand, even if it is only rarely that we glimpse and touch them.

The moment stands alone, and yet it may be the point after which I began to pay attention to magpies and eventually to come to know them as well as any wild or semi-wild creature, to know them as a bird of much intelligence and appetite, both executioner and vulture, a being nearly human in all this but with the added skill of flight: fighter plane of a bird, helicopter gunship of a bird, thing to be both feared and admired.

A pointed black beak of moderate length emerges from a black hood of a head whose feathers drape like a medieval cowl down its back and like a bib down its pure-white breast, a beak that can snap a gosling's neck, beaks that have been known to gang up and kill lambs. Add black eyes whose whitish lids wink in a shuttered flash to the fore-jerk of the head as the bird struts across a lawn; and long black wings with white lozenge-shaped epaulets and flashy white bars, an iridescent black-green, a dark tourmaline, alternating with bands of mat black; with a long tail that serves for braking and balancing and which is carried with feathers bundled together in a narrow band while the bird forages on the ground. In flight the magpie will fan its tail wide in order to slow, to prepare for that stone-like drop to the ground where, hardly pausing, it can spring back up with its powerful legs to resume the straight yet swooping flight which marks it from the curving sweeps of other birds at even great distances.

No bird appears so constantly driven by hunger, particularly once the brood has hatched and the parents must get to work. This takes place in April and May. With few competent enemies, magpies will airlift their cargo of dog food and worms straight to the nest without bothering to set up decoy routes, and their arrival will be accompanied by squawks of me-first desperation by the young. When fully fledged and nearly full-sized, the adolescent birds will move about with their parents yet demand to be fed even when it's apparent they could fend for themselves. They'll stand on the ground or perch on a branch, pull in necks, flutter wings, open beaks, squawk.

The development of intelligence, we are told, seems to require an extended period of juvenile dependency. I have seen—sympathized with—parent birds airlifting massive quantities of insect protein to fully developed young, sleek and fat, well into summer. In autumn and even winter I have seen the young still begging to be fed, at an age that rendered them indistinguishable from the adult birds. You can wonder what all of this intelligence is for. In them. In us. Whatever.

One windy afternoon some years ago our son, Adam, who was eight at the time, brought home a fledgling that had fallen from the nest. It had not yet learned the fear of other creatures and was still innocent, still believed, if that is the word, that any sudden movement within a certain distance of its beak was a signal for it to fling back head, open beak wide, flutter wings, then squawk—in case the three previous signals were ignored. It would hold the open-mouth position for an instant, then revert to a more relaxed and observant state.

At my son's age I knew about cats and dogs of course, and chickens and ducks and geese, and would soon cause the pipelines of the exotic pet industry to pump through our Southern California household a dozen varieties of tropical fish, plus finches, parakeets and a cockatiel, also hamsters and white mice and rats, and horned toads and chameleons and salamanders, very few of which escaped with their lives.

When very young one of the things I did that most haunted me was to move a ladder beneath the hanging nest of a pair of California bushtits, small gray birds that cheepingly work leaves and branches for small insects in the manner of warblers, and which I was quite entranced with; to discover that in filching their tiny eggs I not only rendered them lifeless, whatever my hopes (though this I could have worked out), but that I had also lost the fleeting companionship of the birds themselves when they abandoned the violated nest.

Later, older but no wiser, I stole a fledgling mockingbird from its nest intending to keep it on a leash attached to a lead weight I had devised in advance, but with the usual sad result.

Pets: perhaps they were my first clumsy attempts to grope through the enfolding veils of acculturation in order to know those other worlds, in order to break down the barrier, but without the intelligence yet to comprehend that I was doomed to destroy what I would possess. What the child does not see is that no creature lives without context. And that is what it finally dies for the lack of. Its nest, its air, its earth, its river, its sea. Which growing garlic or farming or any activity with a border open to—I suppose—the universe, or whatever engages you in the contemplation of an ever-expanding sense of context, can finally, if you let it, begin to reveal the boundless extent of.

Friends had long ago raised a magpie. We phoned them. They fussed and groaned. But told us what to feed it—softened dog food, what else?—and warned us that the bird would be like having another child in the house.

And then it would end up getting killed by a car.

Good luck, they said, and hung up.

*

16

HOW TO RAISE A
MAGPIE

THEY WERE RIGHT about most things.

First you will need the cardboard box. This you will put near the heater, to keep the creature warm. Basic stuff.

Allow about a day to master the art of soaking dog food to the right consistency, of fishing out the softened lumps, then of quickly and forcefully stuffing them one at a time down the bird's gullet with an aggressively stiff index finger.

By observing a pair of foraging parent magpies, you can readily estimate that one of the two birds would touch down at the nest every five minutes or so, at least during the more urgent times of the day, which are morning and evening. Two and three young will be fed in this manner.

Your brain may be wracked by thoughts of the bizarreness of the business, of feeding this mixture of slaughterhouse offal and grain and fishery scraps—dolphins? whales?—to a fledgling a thousand miles from the sea, instead of to your dogs and cats, already strange enough: But that is another matter.

After a week or so of such a schedule, your bird will be able to jump out of the box and perch on the edge, which

will usefully—in nature—allow it now and then not to foul
its own nest. Soon it will be able to hop around the house
squawking after you. And soon you will be able to take it
outside and park it in a bush or tree while you go about your
yard and gardening chores. When it begins to struggle from
branch to branch to try to follow you, and when it begins at
last in a crashing way to learn to fly, then it will also assume
the beginnings of what will become a very strong character.
From then on, as usual, you are on your own.

We called him or her—what else?—Maggie. I tended
to think of him as male. Stay-at-home parent, I ended up
becoming his principal feeder and keeper. Having taught
himself to fly, he explored the orchard and trees along the
fences and along the irrigation ditch up behind the house but
always stayed within calling range, as he was still dependent
on being fed, at least some of the time. Eventually he spent
his days outside fending for himself while still insisting on
coming inside at night. If we forgot him, he would fly around
the house at window level until we opened the screen door.
Then he'd swoop across the living room to a turn-of-the-
century ormolu clock that had been a wedding present to my
great aunt Ina and that now sits on the mantelpiece of our
adobe fireplace.

It was Maggie's favorite perch. The clock's two parts
stand on a black enamel base. Left, the tarnished cast-iron
housing for the clockworks, all scroll, pendant, pedestal, handle, knob, and geegaw, with a cream-colored enamel face
behind beveled round glass; and right, the seated figure of a
berobed, long-haired poet with a stylus poised above a word
inscribed on a scroll, sans serif, large caps: ODE. To one side
of the ornate bench upon which he half-reclines, there stands
a basket of scrolls. The ormolu gilt has long since dulled to an
umber brown on both clock housing and poet. A penciled

inscription on the underside records that in 1939 the mechanical works were gutted and replaced by an electric motor.

In the house of my childhood the clock was considered too ugly or old-fashioned for the living room or dining room, and that's how it ended up in my room as one of my prized possessions, and how I came into consciousness and how I slipped into sleep year after year, staring at its ornate mysteries from my bed across from the shelf where it sat. For years I had no idea what an ODE was, what the fellow was up to, what the long hair and beard were about, the scrolls, the basket, what any of this had to do with the telling of time. Now I know. Now I know that the little mysteries presented to you as a child can structure a whole life. At one upswinging moment of my late adolescence, I worked out that the scrolls were writing supplies. Later I understood them as rejects.

The clock now sits on top of the adobe fireplace, eighty or ninety years from the wedding reception and a thousand miles from my childhood room. Unplugged—not because it doesn't work, it does, it keeps excellent time—but because it wheezes, and because I don't want to know the time unless for some reason I decide I need to know the time.

For Maggie, who rode around on my shoulder, on top of my hat or on my head, the resemblance between me and the cast-iron poet may have been obvious. One of us was for day use. The other one was for night use, the one that didn't move around. In this respect Maggie was smarter than me. It has taken several years to parse out the filaments. To follow the bird—or spider—or whatever—into the labyrinth, and then back out. In time Maggie came to bespatter the cast-iron poet with his droppings. This too may be fitting. There are still traces.

Early one morning I found him perched on the windowsill above the kitchen sink, where he stood with a rhine-stone ring in his beak admiring himself in the glass of a round shaving mirror, tipping his head this way and that. The moment he became aware of my presence, he dropped the ring and flew to the door to be let out.

Maggie took a dislike to certain friends of the family, women all, and the moment they walked up the drive or stepped out of their cars he would land on their heads and peck at their hair. Clue perhaps to his sex, if in fact his sex was not something that we somehow imposed on him, igno-rant of our own strange powers. And there were other prob-lems. He regularly raided and fouled a neighbor's outdoor breakfast table. Typical teenage behavior, I supposed. We fretted, apologized. Like having another child in the house, we remembered. A delinquent. He needed to learn. What could Rose Mary and I or even our children teach? How to pick and wash vegetables, how to weed, how to plant—such useless skills for a bird. Yet he would fly down to the field and hover and hop around me while I weeded or pulled beets and carrots or cut lettuce for harvest. And he was a good learner. But he could neither pick nor pull nor cut. Instead, what he could do was peck. And peck he did—at the odd beet, carrot, head of lettuce. And not understand why I would get upset. And no doubt becoming upset himself at the awful flavors of the things he was being shown to peck. And all this took place within the confines of my own shadow, beneath my legs as I crouched, or to one side as I stood. In the high sun of late morning magpies take to the shade. Provider of shade, I was not completely useless.

After we picked—and pecked—we would wash the vegetables in twin tubs set up in the shade of our small apple orchard down from the house, at the end of the lawn. All this was when we were in the early years of our farm life, before garlic had become a major crop. While we were washing the vegetables they were safe from Maggie. We could cull out the ones he had damaged. But then I had to make sure to keep the newly packed boxes covered with a tarp, otherwise Maggie would peck at them too. This was very stressful for us all. However much our restaurant customers might be amused by magpie stories, they still wanted unblemished produce. Afternoons could go better, down at the river, at a pool not far from the bottom of the driveway, where Maggie would fly with us and splash himself in the water, then spread out his wings and tail to dry, feathers ruffled, neck bent over, eyes closed, right next to Rose Mary on the towel, or even on her back if she would let him. He would also bathe himself when I irrigated, despite the fact that his baths rendered him too heavy to fly. In the years since that summer I have only once caught sight of a magpie bathing itself, at the edge of the lawn, just out the living room window, but much more delicately than the wallowing emersions that Maggie must have learned from us.

Toward the middle of the summer our relations deteriorated—as they often will between teenagers and parents, even without species differences. At the end of one long and difficult picking day I lost my patience. Maggie was perched on the open door of the pickup. He had been especially persistent in his peckings. I slammed the door. I had wanted to frighten him away with the noise. But he hung on. The door caught one of his feet. It was a terrible instant. I wrenched the door open, releasing the fluttering bird. He flew off.

He remained lame in one foot. We began to see less of him. Not because of the accident, or so I hoped. When he was still being fed by us other magpies would pay quick, curious visits, then fly off, as if to check for themselves what magpie gossip was reporting down at the river. Later he began to spend more time with his true kin. The change coincided with that time of mid-summer when magpies all gather together and fly briefly as a flock, which perhaps serves to loosen the parental bond or which is part of a mating ritual in which the gene pool is once again stirred. Molting begins after flocking time. Magpies will then remain shy and retiring during the loss and replacement of their sleek plumage. They need not much exert themselves, given the late summer abundance of grasshoppers and other large insects. You will see little of them. Occasionally a droopy, moth-eaten black-and-white bird will hop down to the edge of a field, then fly away into the shadows.

Maggie disappeared during flocking time. To join his peers, I would like to think. He was smart enough to know that it was time to cut the awkward and dangerous ties with his monstrous foster parents. In the fall, a month or two later, a magpie lame in one foot took to approaching a little closer than you might expect and would sometimes sit in a nearby tree muttering away to itself at great length while I worked in the field.

Perhaps it was Maggie, perhaps not. In solitary moments magpies will perch on a branch and mutter soft soliloquies of whines and squeals and chatterings, oblivious to what goes on around them. It is one of those things, I suppose, intelligence now and then does, must in fact now and then do, must think, must play, must imagine, must talk to itself.

But since those days in August when he was last with us nearly fifteen years ago, no magpie has flown to me in that enthralling way Maggie often did at my call, from a distant tree or bush: he would aim straight at the level of my eyes and then, tail flashing wide, brake and rise at the last instant to alight on top of my head. I still remember that beak pointing toward me in flight, those large liquid eyes, all bobbing up and down as propelled closer and closer by rising and falling wings.

This story has nothing to do with my relations with garlic. Other than that I discovered something about the wind and the sky, the shape of that fluid space that hovers over and sweeps across and around my labors, and of which in my land-boundness I would know so much less had it not been for the efforts of a creature blown out of a tree by the wind to recover, however roundabout the way—the hands of a child, a cardboard box, an old clock—or however extravagant the means—a family of loud, inept humans—to regain the context he had lost.

What, finally, intelligence could be for: finding your way back.

17

ACCRETIONS

OTHER FIELD CROPS GROW faster and more aggressively than garlic.

This may not be to its disadvantage. In nature we can assume that garlic's strategy is to secure a niche both in space, where it seems to prefer damp and even shady ground, and in time, when it will produce most of its growth in the cooler parts of the seasons. Its bulb, its secret underground defense system, its storage warehouse of energy for future growth, is what allows the plant to wait out the months of rampant growth by surrounding annual plants and even deciduous shrubs and trees. While they seek light and sun, garlic reposes in the cool of the earth; and when the shortening days and cooling nights of autumn redirect the growth of more tender plants into stems and seeds and roots, garlic reads the signal in the opposite sense, as an all-clear, as time to emerge, as time to root, as time to catch its ration of sunlight before all is overgrown again.

The arrangement works fine in nature—or rather in the semi-wild state. Witness the competitive landscape of an orchard, where in the company of a half-dozen types of grass garlic can survive in the shade of a well-watered apple tree, where it is trampled and mowed and even parked on—but if you dig up the bulbs, if you break into the garlic ghettos, you will find few cloves big enough to take up to the kitchen, though large enough apparently to sustain the plant through its dormancy period.

An object of cultivation is to reduce the size and quantity of weeds in order to increase the size of the bulb or fruit or stalk or root of your crop. This is mostly what "growing"—what people do to make things grow—consists of, of eliminating everything else that gets in the way. But garlic is not one of your desperate, grasping crops that try to reach everywhere and cover everything by the end of the season, like tomatoes or pumpkins. You can sometimes think that garlic doesn't really care whether you cultivate it or not. It can manage by itself, thank you. And indeed it can, if you are content with small bulbs of four or five cloves.

For something larger, for a plump, fully developed bulb, you will need to cultivate, which you may begin as soon as you can see to do so, as soon as enough garlic leaves have thrust through the surface to mark the rows. In a northern climate, this is likely to be from the beginning of March onward. No need for the tractor at first: a leisurely scuffle-shuffle with a sharpened hoe will easily uproot fall-seeded clumps of grass which, if left a month longer, will take two or three energetic whacks to dig up. The very perennial grasses that later seem to crowd the garlic's niche may also serve, from the garlic view, to keep the ground cool during the long passage through hot summer days. My first late-winter or early-spring task after trolling up cottonwood and willow roots along the verges will be to cruise the garlic fields on foot in search of garlic's grassy companions. It limbers me up. For years I turned the work over to my seasonal right-hand man on the farm, Lawrence Lucero, until I realized I needed the exercise after three or four months of sedentary living. I also needed to reacquaint myself with my fields, and this is best done by foot, row by row, over the course of several mornings or afternoons.

The winter freezings and thawings will have rumpled up the soil and broken up clods, making it resemble the surface of a cookie or a loaf of French bread or something else out of the oven, with the soil cast into small rolled shapes by the convulsions of the weather; and it will appear as less a terrestrial landscape than something in miniature you might expect to find on another planet. A crust will have formed. It will hold moisture yet also retard germination of smaller seeds and even prove an obstacle to garlic that attempts to emerge during an early spring dry spell, and beneath the plates of hardening soil here and there you will find blanched and folded leaves waiting to be released by rain or the slicings of a hoe.

So I move through the fields with a hoe, often covering two and three rows at a time, flipping the tussocks of grass over on their backs, roots skyward, to keep them from re-rooting, should a rain soon come. The fields seem relatively lifeless, beyond the bright green shoots tinged with red that mark my path. But I have learned that this work, which I used to put off until much too late, takes so little time that I now look forward to the early March mornings and the exhilarating air, still crisp, even cold; and once done, I'm free of the fields for a month or so, until the first tractor cultivation—or so I can tell myself.

The reality may be closer to a week. One task completed opens the door to the next. Because the soil is drying out, it follows that I'll soon have to irrigate, which reminds me that I'll need to clean out my ditches, those two-shovel wide channels that run down along the driveways of two of my fields. Their grassy banks must be dug back each year and trimmed of last season's growth of willow canes and cotton-wood suckers, plum and bush cherry, and the silt and sand and dead leaves scraped off the bottom—in order to receive the first water from the acequia, the community irrigation ditch, when its two miles of channel are dug out toward the end of March.

These first tasks of late winter mark the shift from waiting, from enfolding myself with great wrappings of time, from that state in which the easeful thinking through of tasks and processes becomes reconverted into that suddenly time-devouring reality of doing, acting, laboring, and the always unplanned-for need to rest, or not just rest, but to rest more. I would take great pleasure in this modest ditch-cleaning work were I not by then always hurried—and overexcited by the list of spring chores re-forming in my mind—and were I not nagged at by the wind while driving a winter-stiff body to bend and swivel again, crouch and reach.

One of these ditches, at the house, I must clear by hand without the help of tractor and blade, because I have planted it with lilac, ash, and Russian olive, and chokecherry has sprung up of its own accord, all to form a long variegated north-south border along our east fenceline that I am inordinately fond of. The narrow channel must be carefully dug out each spring, otherwise the irrigation water will flow over its raised banks to flood our driveway or the place next door. So it is rake, prune, dig for two afternoons or so, usually in the wind, as I snake my way through the tight spaces between trunks and branches and the barbed-wire fence, down the narrow channel barely wide enough to walk and dig in. The rakings go into the compost heap, the prunings down to a bank along the river where I pile them in order to slow erosion, and the silt and sand serve to raise the banks of the channel a little higher each year.

When you stay in one place for a while, the accretions of small labors such as this begin to show as gradual change, like the growth of trees. Twenty years ago there was nothing along our east fence except sagging, rusting strands of barbed wire strung along gray juniper posts. Now there stands a row of thirty-foot trees thrusting up out of a raised bank of earth a foot and a half high and cut down its center by the winding irrigation channel. Likewise an abandoned headgate tells me that the banks of the main irrigation ditch, the acequia, up behind the house, are a foot higher than they were twenty years ago and that the bottom of the channel is some six inches lower, all through the labors of some twenty-five men and boys passing through with shovels once a year, west to east.

I find these slow changes through accretion and wear sources of quiet gratification—a way to sense perhaps the nature of the infinitesimal alterations over the millennia that have changed the face of the earth as much as the grand upheavals. The wear of roads and paths, the grinding up of stone into gravel and sand, sand into silt, of roots and branches worn smooth by tumbling rides in rivers down from the mountains, or the way flowing water polishes stones or roughens cement or raises the grain of boards; and then those liquid accretions of snow and rain, and how the wind sculpts the sand and clay of the cliffs: I take pleasure in observing effects which proceed by bits, by motes, by almost intangible degrees, and which are analogous, I suppose, to the more dramatic changes in vegetative growth, however slow even these last may seem to our heartbeat clocks— changes triggered and fed by accretions of light and, if one can so speak, of darkness itself.

I find these slow changes, or the ones I am an agent of, gratifying in part because I know some of the silt dug out from the ditches will find its way down into the garden and the fields. In summer I'll often put on rubber boots and climb down into the flowing water of the acequia and stir up the muck, in order to make it sluice out my headgate into the ditches and rows of my field, moving perhaps several hundred pounds of nutrient-laden silt at a time—but whose effects I may be unable to perceive for many years. The growth of trees, the eating away and building up of banks, those slower changes of nature can be best savored by the frequenters of one place—the shifting course of a river or an arroyo, the patches of wear on a floor or sill, the slow wearing away of the metal of a hoe until it is a thin, light blade, until it becomes the extension of arm and hand and fingers, a blade in which you can feel, as you file it sharp each morning, the harder and softer bands of iron where the annealing has held or failed—until it becomes too small and too light as a blade, without enough heft to cut through the stalks and roots of larger weeds.

Your hoe and your shovel become comfortable only in time, like old clothes, and when finally they wear too thin through tens of thousands of strokes through the earth, putting them aside for the new tool, heavy and awkward, is one of those small difficult moments. I find it hard to throw the old ones away, and they lie scattered around the outside of the shed with their light-reflecting blades turned brown with rust, as if waiting for a new use that will polish them with labor again.

You will see this on the acequia, during the annual digging late in March: the young men with their heavy new shovels bought the morning before at the local store, tools that will squander their strength over the course of a day or two of digging; and the old men with theirs, implements worn to some small thin shape, handles deep with weathered cracks, often taped, and which they wield with the precision of surgical instruments. To watch them dig, or to watch them hoe in their chile patches, is to believe this is easy work. And in a sense it is. With decades of practice they have made it so, having learned how to avoid showing signs of aches and pains any of these movements may set off in their bodies, and how not to waste their motions. All is work, or all is rest.

When we built the first two rooms of our adobe house twenty some years ago, one of the last tasks was to lay an adobe floor in the living room. We did it late and badly and laid it too thick. The mud dried slowly, and wide cracks opened up, which we have patched and sealed over the years, often hastily and fretfully—to arrive at the strange point of possessing a floor we could not have created any other way, a surface that resembles a giant slab of flagstone that has been weathered and beaten by the elements, with all the faults and irregularities that only wear and stress can create, not design: a surface into which I pour my thoughts and dreams, and across which I pace, a field of introspection which my very thought serves in its way to wear and polish. In a time when so many manufactured objects do not wear well—they are new and shiny and then dull and scratched, faded and cracked with little transition—I take pleasure in the wear of things of wood and stone and earth, even of iron, cloth, leather; in wear that is a kind of growth, if you stretch the notion far enough.

And awareness of this can perhaps be read as a sign of the degree to which we feel at home in a place, and can also be the beginnings of the acceptance of the final knowledge that we will eventually become part of the granular matter underfoot, of ash settling down from the sky, of silt being swept down streams and ditches, the sweeping waters themselves, if we stay anywhere long enough. Which, finally, somewhere, we have to, on the way to rejoining the grand accretion of everywhere.

※

18

CHEATGRASS

Cheatgrass is another matter.

On my first walks with a hoe up and down the rows I will have noticed—lazily, complacently—patches of short dark greenish blades with a reddish tinge, thin scatterings not enough to hoe, sproutings like stands of mold growing out of an old piece of bread. Perhaps I'll give them a swipe or two and make a mental note to come back in a week or so and deal with them properly.

A clever organism, a grassy weed, *Bromus tectorum*, it knows us and all our negligences in garden and field. It knows our habits and is well aware of our inherent laziness and of our frequent unwillingness to bestir ourselves too early in the spring or even too late in the fall, and it knows of our weakness for fire. I sometimes think it even knows that it should hold back until after I have walked through my fields and hoed out the more abundant clumps of perennial grasses.

Cheatgrass reveals itself as the first emerald green patches growing along the borders of fields and paths and roads and ditches, which is to say those spaces we use in an occasional way without actually occupying. The plant knows we'll tolerate its presence on our verges and won't really

claim the borders and ditch banks and driveways, or at least
not in time, not early enough. Its strategy is of those who
work early and rapidly and then rest while the remainder of
the world labors under the hot sun. It will often get a good
start in the fall, or a seemingly modest start, nothing to concern yourself about, an attractive dense weave of bright green
in patches at either end of a field, an adornment to a landscape turning to gold, rust, gray. And then with cold weather
the thin blades—no clumps yet—turn a protective dark green
with a faint reddish tinge which they hold until spring.

Cheatgrass spends a certain effort, if those are the
terms, trying to convince us that it is not very important. As
grasses grow, it rarely exceeds a foot in height. Its blades seem
frail, pull out easily—like the tails of certain lizards—leaving
the matted roots intact in the ground. But by the time most
people are ready to plant their gardens, cheatgrass may already
have matured and sent up its first seed stalks, often on the
strength of only the lightest rain, and will be preparing to
retire for the season. Or, if the rains are abundant, it will
establish itself even better, waiting until a long dry spell before
heading up. Either way it has won its ground until late
August or early September, when the rains return and the
weather begins to cool again. Its quickness and tenacity and
adaptability seem to mock the ponderous labors of the farmer
who is bound up with fastidious notions of planting evenly
spaced seeds in rows so many feet apart.

Most mulches serve to conserve moisture. Cheatgrass
is what I would call a negative mulch, a monopolizing ground
cover that seems to work at rendering the soil too dry for any
other species to gain a toehold. Moisture-loving garlic is particularly susceptible, and more so in a light or shallow soil that
will not hold much moisture anyway. Once it has seeded and
dried up, cheatgrass's mass of dry roots and leaves and its short

dry golden stalks serve to ventilate the moisture out of the soil, holding the patch in reserve for the late summer or early fall rains, when the fast-sprouting seeds can reclaim the earth ahead of anything else. The stalks are extremely flammable, which assures a rapid and thus relatively cool burn that will not consume the seeds that have dropped into cracks in the earth, deep within the matted cover of fine, dry leaves— though you will hear the ones that have not made it to safety exploding with little pops in the flames. When dry, cheatgrass almost seems to invite fire, to invite you to bring out the matches and drag out the garden hose and do a little burning off, which is just how you can best assure its perpetuation— with the potash-fertilizing shortcut that fire provides. After a fire, the first thing up is cheatgrass. Clever plant. See, its innumerable blades of emerald green seem to be saying, I'm back. In one way or another you can easily fall into its long-laid trap year after year.

Several years back our foothill valley experienced a particularly wet spring that produced thick stands of cheatgrass along the edges of roads and in neglected fields and backyards. Then in May the weather turned hot and dry; the cheatgrass dried out. Then the winds blew. As a result, whenever some sixteen-year-old staying home from school was gruffly told to clean up the dry weeds in the yard, the volunteer fire department would be inevitably summoned to put out a west-to-east running inferno that threatened houses and orchards and the woods lining the river, the *bosque* lands of cottonwood and willow. It was the worst fire season in years.

One of the local gossip mills is operated by the under-employed, the unemployed, the never-employed, the early retired, the stay-at-homes, a largely male group I may possibly have earned honorary membership in. Its sessions are largely conducted during breaks in the two- and three-day-long digging out of the acequias in the spring. This particular group advanced the ingenious theory that the Federal Government had secretly seeded the grass as part of some experiment, or as its latest assault upon the integrity of the village, upon its property boundaries or grazing lands or water rights or wood-gathering customs or its share of food stamps or welfare or Medicare benefits or surplus food commodities. The less-educated people of the village maintain a special relationship with the President of the United States: they blame him personally for the little things that go wrong. Thus they all knew that then-President Ronald Reagan somehow had a hand in the fires.

But little wonder. The atomic bomb was invented forty-five miles away. Nobody knew about it until afterward. Not until the war was over were the roads paved and the first Hispanic people from the village began working in numbers up in Los Alamos, where they were hauled in the back of an enclosed flatbed truck heated by a wood stove in the winter. Even in those years, what you saw in Los Alamos did not correspond in any logical way to the devastation planned there for the rest of the world. This no doubt gave rise to the inventive rumor that there is another Los Alamos, a vast subterranean city carved out of the volcanic froth underlying the town and laboratory, a super-secret metropolis nobody ever talks about.

Cheatgrass—if I correctly follow the reasoning that attempted to link the fires and the government and the Los Alamos National Laboratory—would probably be the first thing up after a potash-releasing nuclear holocaust, the first plant to reclaim the earth. Hence suspicions of secret seedings and official arson, all bizarrely consistent, as part of some elaborate test for the next secret weapon.

But in my experience cheatgrass hardly needs government assistance in claiming its territory. The plant's spring emergence, or rather its first aggressive growth, presents an early problem of the new season. To become aware of a thriving patch of it is almost simultaneously to surrender to it. Even my geese cannot keep up. The plant's habit of generating thick masses of fine roots makes cultivating or tilling almost futile. In order to keep ahead, you must uproot it while the weather is often too cold to work with bare hands—or at a time when there are competing claims to prune the trees, clean out the irrigation ditches, plant the greenhouse, ready the machinery for spring planting. Too often over the years I have watched a patch or strip of cheatgrass suck the moisture out of the end of a row and strangle whatever I have planted there, to triumph in a stand of low drooping seed heads that look like poor cousins of oats.

And these too are confident of what they're about. They stand ankle-high as if they know all about woolly socks, cuffs, boots, and the fur of small curly-haired dogs. As they dry up, and as you stride through their stands or whack them down or till them under, the seeds will cling to socks, drop into cuffs, will even somehow find their way down into the fingers of gloves and the depths of pockets. The pointed casings feature a sharp end that will easily penetrate a loose weave and even work its way into the seams of canvas shoes. And so it must know how we will sooner or later go home and how we'll empty our shoes, pockets, and gloves outside the front door—thus sowing a future mat of cheatgrass conveniently close to a rich source of foot traffic.

And there it waits at the fringes of our seasons, of our labors, in those little deserts we create for each other, and where it pretends most of the time that it is dead and dying, as a patch of dry grass that we'll leave neglected, which we'll now and then back into or turn around or park on or walk across. Cheatgrass waits there with the patience, with the always secret hope of being able to take over the whole field during a fallow year, a field that, sooner or later, through neglect or through holocaust, will be offered up to it.

Inventive antagonist: yet also a clock by which I measure the end of winter and the approach of spring, and whose alarm sounds louder and louder, to remind me that the long wait is over and that the time has come again to move out into the elements.

✳

III
SPRING:
CONTEXTS

※

19

WATER: CONTINUED

STRANGERS WHO WANDER up the drive in late March or early April will gesture toward the garlic patch.

"Is that corn?" they'll ask—incredulously or absently, depending on their remove from such matters.

The error is understandable. A patch of newly emerging garlic can seem to resemble corn, except the color is too blue-green and the flat leaves are a little too narrow. And of course you would not see six-inch-high corn for another month or two.

Other than winter wheat or rye a field of garlic will be the greenest thing around at the end of March. Dig up one of the scallion-like plants and you will find a mass of silvery white roots radiating out into the soil. This is why you want to plant in the fall, not spring: to gain that foot of overall growth in roots and leaves that you cannot obtain by holding the bulbs in storage over winter.

There is something startling about such abundant growth so early, a month or so before most trees have begun to leaf out, before the garden has been tilled or planted, before most of the annual weeds have even sprouted. Now is when garlic makes a run for it. Solar rights are there for the asking, with little competition. The plant can also slough off the late snows and last frosts which can persist into May. Garlic thrives in those gaps that open up at the borders of the seasons, in the intervals when the calendar seems out of step with the weather, when spring still seems to be winter, when days lengthen faster than the earth can warm, and in the shrinking yet still summery days of mid-autumn.

Late autumn and early spring are also times when the ground is likely to be damp close to the surface. In northern New Mexico, however, soil moisture often begins to withdraw in early spring beyond the reach of garlic's shallow roots. Snows and rains are often erratic and not to be depended on. Soon I will need to irrigate, usually in April for the first time, and often late in March.

I irrigate infrequently in the new season at first, once a month or so, in the field at the house, or up the road, or across the river. Then as the days lengthen and warm, I'll irrigate once every two weeks. Then through the long rainless stretches of late spring and early summer, once a week will become the norm, up until the moment I begin drying out the garlic fields.

Most of my feeder ditches run south down alongside driveways, perpendicular to the acequia, to divide themselves further into successions of secondary ditches that feed ten to twenty furrows each, running west and following thus the general east-west slope of the land. Small steel headgates release water from the acequia, which is then distributed to the secondary ditches by means of gates or obstructions improvised out of pipe, boards, rocks and tussocks of grass, woven plastic sacks, patches of plastic sheeting. Once you have your ditches set up right, irrigation is largely a matter of leaning on a shovel and watching water, a poet's work.

There are of course better ways to do all this. Wells,

pumps, gated pipe, drip irrigation systems, whatever. All of which, capital once invested, can claim to be more efficient and productive than traditional methods of irrigation.

There are two considerations. One has to do with the aesthetics of what I do. I farm—a kind of painting on earth, a kind of writing on earth—because of the constantly changing patterns I can create with water, seed, soil, sunlight, the weather. The memories of what I have made, the visions of what I hope to bring into existence, and the image of narrow channels of water winding their way through the back yards of my small valley: these are what most deeply motivate me.

The other has to do with the social, with community, with human borders, with the acequia. Invitations to seek private satisfaction or consolation or wealth or power come relentlessly to us in these times, at the expense almost always of the public and the communal, whose invitations are weak and uncertain and filled with doubt, and lacking in the high-budget promotional certainties of the age. Were Ford or General Motors selling community, not fantasies of power and mobility, we might be living in quite a different world.

The water I take such pleasure in, in the furrow, in the acequia, in the river, is mine only in a transitory and heavily mediated way: it is delivered for my use, for my pleasure, through the labors of my thirty land-owning neighbors and the indirect consent of everybody else who irrigates in this small valley.

For a long time I ignored the implications of the fact. I was among those who fled to the country and went into farming to get away from it all, out of notions of independence and self-sufficiency and out of an impulse to escape the complex burden of the social.

Much of farming can be as solitary as you want—or simply lonely—in degrees that are often proportionate to the

[105]

amount of equipment you own. The more you own, the less you need the help of others. Or rather, because you employ the assistance of others in the form of machinery and tools which are invented, designed, manufactured by others, you need much less of these others as people. Thus you will not have them hanging around as contentious living presences all too willing to dispute your view of life and the world.

Some calculations are in order. To begin with there are those thirty other families, my neighbors on the acequia, whose help I need to irrigate my garlic fields. Further: to help with planting and cultivating and fertilizing the garlic, I need one or two part-time workers throughout the season. For harvest, add another dozen friends and workers each year, some paid, some not, for the three-morning task.

To process the harvested crops, garlic and statice flowers in particular, Rose Mary and I need three and sometimes four people working half-time over the course of about four months in the summer.

To sell what we produce—what family and workers and friends produce—requires the further collaboration of the three families with whom we share our retail space in Taos. Plus the volunteer assistance of the groups that run the markets in Santa Fe and Los Alamos. Plus, obviously, the two thousand or so customers each spending ten to twenty dollars a season on garlic, flowers, onions, basil, lettuce, gourds, to help pay our costs for materials and labor and to some small degree compensate us for our time.

Organizing a landscape into an agricultural purpose, even a small one of six or seven acres, is no solitary labor. Of necessity it is a pre-eminently cooperative and social one, even in the heart of a nation awash in the media myths of self-sufficiency and rugged individualism.

20

AN ORCHARD,
A PAINTING

SOME YEARS AGO a painter friend set up his easel on our lawn and set about painting the orchard, or more exactly a scene that included the small stone tower Rose Mary and I had built as my writing studio to the left, and to the right the trestle table where we washed vegetables for market in the shade, and to the foreground, under an apple tree, our green and white Chevy pickup waiting to be loaded.

The scene he chose was a foreshortened and contracted version of what you glimpse out the living room window. From here, in summer, the apple orchard stands against a taller backdrop of light green cottonwoods lining the river, and a half-mile beyond them, the long bluff that marks the southern boundary of the valley.

I pondered his labors from time to time whenever I rested from my own. My usual resting place is an armchair in front of the living room window.

The armchair, a Victorian piece in maroon velours, was once my grandfather's, as were the two totems brought down from Sitka ninety years ago and which now stand on the windowsill, watching too through the glass: bear, eagle, mosquito, seal.

Resting, staring out the window: staring through glass I had puttied into frames I had built myself. Frames set in flared window casings I had built with the help of my father. Casings set in an adobe wall that friends and family had helped lay up, plaster, paint. I watched the painter standing in the afternoon sun, halfway down the lawn, midway between my armchair and where we would soon resume our work washing and packing vegetables.

I began to see what any painter would have to leave out in the schematizing process of two-dimensional representation, in order to produce a two-foot by three-foot token of something I knew to be immeasurably vaster and more complex.

Not to be seen were generation after generation of human hands that had grafted scion to root stock to convey that half-natural, half-cultural creation, the apple tree, through the millennia to this valley, across ocean and continent.

Nor the accumulated weight of all that I bore to this patch of ground, or that Rose Mary bore, and that had driven us to build that tower, plant this lawn, till the field beyond the apple trees; nor the freight of time and history that had transported so much else, even some of the very weeds, to this apparently middle-of-nowhere place, at this apparently ordinary and unremarkable moment. These other dimensions were to be absent from the painting, they would drop away or more properly could never be there, except if brought to its lines and pigments by one who had acquired the memory of all of this.

Something flipped over. As when you discover that you know much more than you thought you did, even though it may be insignificant in relation to all that could be known, even about a small place.

We see the leaves, the branches, the flowers, the stalks. But foundations, the roots and the bulbs, we must mostly imagine, and the social structures that underlie even our most basic labors. Indeed our pleasure and happiness may often lie in such sweeping denials.

Notions of self-sufficiency had guided me in part to this place, to do this or that thing, to grow gardens and then crops, to become a grower of garlic—notions which I have since packed away somewhere or have hung up on a wall and which, when I now and then notice them, can give me momentary pleasure, even relief, like a painting of a wooded landscape with open fields—until I recall myself to the bewildering context that frames all endeavors large or small, solitary or social.

The painting that would reveal this landscape would be like one of those crowded group photos—a family reunion in a park, say—with hundreds or even thousands of people, the old and the young, the living and their memories and ghosts, all of whom have had a hand in what can appear, from a certain angle, at certain moments, to be only a quiet landscape of trees and open ground.

⁂

21

WATER: CONCLUDED

THE ACEQUIA GIVES me water. Like my neighbors I have labored for it in various ways. I have served as one of the acequia's elected commissioners for most of the past twenty years and as its *mayordomo* or ditch boss for the rest.

I also carry a certain baggage to the acequia. These are the old suitcases I open up whenever I think about water, about race and culture and language, about the real. Everyone of course lugs such baggage around, even the children of wolves. Even my own children. Even children who supposedly have been raised to be completely free of it, and perhaps especially them.

I have spent a lot of time figuring out how I got to this particular here of all places, and doing this particular that, of all things. In a mobile society, such thinking may even be a national pastime. No logic other than that of childhood dreams and fears could anticipate the steps that led my wife and I from opposite ends of the earth to meet and then to live this particular life together: to grow an Asian crop in the territory once claimed by the Picuris Pueblo, then by the Kingdom of Spain, then by Mexico, now by the United States, in a Hispanic village where former enemies and persecutors have allied themselves, if often warily, to form a kind of ramshackle community.

But if you can bear to cling to them, such complexities may serve to keep you honest and thus out of the grip of the fanatical certainties. And the borders of language and culture and race stay down because they must be crossed each day again, in each encounter on the banks of the acequia and at the post office and at the store. Or each time I walk in the door of the adobe house a Hispanic village taught a California gringo how to build.

I carry all this to the village and to the acequia, as baggage I hope someday to be able to lay down or at least become indifferent to—when time has made me as much a creature of this place, of its fields and ditches, of its water, as those who were born here, as much as my Protestant childhood, that other tidal pull, will allow.

So we work together, young and old, out there on the ditch, some vague sheltering notion of community, guided by customs invented by Moors and imported by Spaniards and grafted on to Pueblo Indian ways. We do not quite know how to celebrate these matters. One of the traditions of the acequia is to complain about it, perhaps as a way to turn away from something men are not supposed to be sensitive to—the beauty of its winding channel, the felicity of flowing waters. But for the past twenty years, for two and three days in late March or early April, I have seen acts of homage that are far more real than mere words—in the actual cutting back of brush and digging out the channel, in the yearly labor that allows the acequia to flow again. Then the water comes down the narrow winding channel through the still-leafless cottonwoods and willows, to the small fields where my garlic lies in wait for the first irrigation. Often the weather will be cold and windy, and it will be odd to be out there that first time in heavy jacket and gloves, moving the muddy water down the feeder ditches with rake and shovel, into the top of the field, sending it down the 150-foot-long rows.

I will squint into the afternoon sun to see how the water is progressing down the furrows and to make out where it has reached the end. I will dig little dams with the tip of my shovel, nudging small stones and clods and tussocks of grass and clumps of dried weeds to slow or cut off the flow. It is all second nature to me now, to pass an afternoon walking back and forth, to set and reset the water on the rows. This solitary and almost eventless labor is the final result of that flurry of social activity by which we clean out the acequia each year, guided by traditions strong enough to cross an ocean and jump borders of language and religion, and a multitude of barriers of individualistic pride.

The water that fingers its way down my 120 rows of garlic, plants ultimately as alien as myself, as alien as most of us to this or any place, is the final and almost trivial effect of vast conquests and migrations, disasters and triumphs. This is the momentum, the human gravity that drives the thin tracks of water down the acequia, the feeder ditches, the furrows of my fields. For myself much of the time, and perhaps for most people, this force lies secretly within the seas of language we skim across in our waking and dreaming lives, and within our very beings, and up from which a fragment of something, seeming to be almost meaningless, will now and then bubble to glint in the sun.

Water percolating down into the earth, bathing the roots, dissolving manure, troubling gophers, drowning worms; water turning the surface of the dry tan soil to a rich brown mud. As it puddles and then slowly sinks into the earth, passing out of the atmospheric realm and leaving a dark path edged with foam—here may be an image of the mechanism by which all things and all beings encounter and dissolve into each other, and thus explanation enough for the improbabilities that might lead anyone to stand with a shovel at the head of a row of green points on a windy afternoon, in a narrow valley in northern New Mexico.

✳

22

FERTILIZERS

GARLIC IS A HEAVY FEEDER, and it will need to be fertilized at planting time and then again in the spring.

For the home gardener with a small patch of garlic, a few sacks of commercially packaged manure or a small pickup load will suffice. For the larger grower, however, fertilizer can easily become a major and even obsessional problem. No thought, other than weed control or irrigation, aspects of the same thing, occupies me so much as the question of when and how much to feed my garlic. As is proper, I suppose, when we raise anything, children, pets, livestock, because feeding is what we hover most solicitously over.

I began as an "organic" gardener. The main value of the organic movement was not so much its philosophy of no chemical pesticides, herbicides, or synthetic fertilizers, as the door it opened for me into gardening and small-scale farming in the sixties and seventies. Turn the pages of *Organic Gardening and Farming* magazine (as it was then called) and it was clear that all you needed was a patch of land, a shovel, hoe, garden fork, some seeds, and you were in business.

In my early organic days I dribbled cottonseed meal down the garlic planting furrows, ladling the orange powder out of a five-gallon bucket as I walked. At the time cottonseed meal was being widely touted by the organic press. I was also fertilizing our garden patch with goat manure from our own animals, but there wasn't enough to cover our acre of garlic and the two or three acres of other crops, mainly corn, that we were also growing. As a sole fertilizer, you need to spread up to ten tons per acre each year. This was more than I could manage with my equipment, supposing I could have found that much in one place and figured out how to load and haul it. Though still bulky, cottonseed meal, banded down rows at planting time and then later again as a side-dressing, provided as much nitrogen and phosphorus as many times the weight of broadcast manure—and was considered organic too, at least for a time. True, I much preferred mucking around in the rich springy deposits of the goat pen to gagging on the orange powder, but cottonseed meal was faster to apply and easier on the back.

But all shortcuts, all conveniences, have problems. Cottonseed meal is sold mainly as an animal feed supplement. Cotton is a crop that can be more heavily treated with pesticides and herbicides than humanly edible crops. I began to wonder how much of such residues might be concentrated in the seed.

What is at issue in agricultural ideologies often has to do with something more like religion than science. My suspicions were enough to eventually doom my use of the fertilizer. I was too willing to confess my worries at the farmers' market about the purity of any method of farming, to the alarm of my more fanatical customers. Cheerful assurances are always preferred, even if they become contradictory over time. I was soon to have a parallel experience with official enthusiasms over sewage sludge, until problems surfaced concerning dangerous concentrations of heavy metals in the soil.

All fertilizers come with worries. If no human activity is ever entirely pure, with questions of fertilizer we're in the deepest possible trouble. Nor are these simply problems for farmers. Eating, as Wendell Berry points out, is an agricultural act. Everyone who eats is involved in these questions.

After rejecting cottonseed meal and sewage sludge I was ripe to be swayed by the argument that chemical fertilizers are "clean," that is, free of pesticide and herbicide and other unwanted residues. Furthermore, superphosphate is a "natural" substance, phosphate rock, treated with sulfuric acid to make it more soluble and thus readily available to the plant. Urea is a soluble compound whose nitrogen is chemically no different from that found in any other form. The main argument of the synthetic fertilizer industry is that an element is an element. It is not entirely without merit, as far as it goes.

I began using synthetic fertilizers and continued to do so until recently, becoming less "organic" in the process—or by the stricter schools of thought not organic at all. My method was to dribble superphosphate, plus some urea, down the irrigation furrow in the fall; this would then be mixed into the soil in the course of putting in and then covering the planting furrow a foot to either side. For phosphorus, this was a less than ideal method of application, since it is a relatively insoluble element and needed to be placed below the roots, not to one side. But as a slowly released element, it would end up where it was supposed to be over the years, thus becoming available to the plants—or so I estimated. Later, in the spring, I would apply a side dressing or two of urea before cultivation, at a time when the plants needed nitrogen for leafy growth.

At the same time I turned to synthetic fertilizer I began to wonder what I could do with the fields in the way of producing a green manure crop between the time we pulled the garlic in July and replanted in late September. These are prime solar energy months. Sun falling on a barren field produces only heat and dust. Most annual grains, like oats, wheat, rye, as well as the legumes, alfalfa, field peas, and the clovers and vetches, are cool-season crops; sharing the same preference as garlic, they want to be planted in the fall or early spring, not in the heat of summer. I had already learned to use winter rye or wheat to follow corn, squash, gourds, and on the fields I rotated out of garlic, and it is now rare that I let any area pass through the winter without a growth of wheat or rye on it, other than the garden patch where we'll be harvesting carrots and parsley well into November. Buckwheat turned out to be the summer green manure crop I was looking for. Its black triangular seeds readily germinate in the warm earth to produce a dense three-foot stand of succulent plants with broad leaves, white flowers and reddish stems, and all in about six weeks. The tender stems and leaves rototill under easily, even when mature, an additional benefit.

Garlic does not respond to fertilizing ministrations as dramatically as corn or squash. Eventually I began to question how much good the urea and superphosphate were doing. The very solubility of the former, generally thought of as a virtue, could serve too rapidly to leach its nitrogen content down beyond the reach of the garlic roots and into our shallow ground water as nitrate pollution, though it is said that green manuring will among other things serve to tie up the soluble nitrogen and hold it in place in the upper levels of the soil where it will become available to the next crop. But I was worried that I was still pulling more out of the soil than I was putting back in, which a decline in the size of our harvest seemed to confirm.

Coincidentally I became aware of the fact that there were loaders and dump trucks in the area. Their owners were willing to transport manure at a price I could afford. In the mountain villages fifteen miles above our valley and a thousand feet higher, many Hispanic families still keep small herds of cattle and sheep. Not much can be grown at seven and eight thousand feet other than pasture—and garlic. That was one source of manure. Another was an organic egg operation that had recently opened near Taos. Within a year its tens of thousands of hens were producing large quantities of manure mixed with a litter of feathers and sawdust, and it was for sale at a reasonable price.

I began moving back toward fully organic methods about three years ago. Most of the manure is now applied in the autumn as part of the planting process, which adds to the time it has to break down and enrich the soil. After tilling under the buckwheat in September, there are two more steps before planting. First, furrowing, in which the furrows are deeply and roughly made by twin shovels mounted on the toolbar and following in the tracks of the tractor. Second, bedshaping, in which the irregular, cloddy furrows are smoothed and shaped and made shallower and more regular, packing down the earth in the process and thus enabling the planter wheels to obtain traction.

Between furrowing and bedshaping, I hitch up the rear fork lift and carry a large three-sided plywood box with a capacity of perhaps fifteen hundred pounds over to the manure pile, where I fill it with manure using the tractor loader. Then I slip the fork lift under the box and fill up the loader bucket one last time and move the laden tractor out into the newly furrowed rows. In this way I can carry up to a ton of manure at a time out into a field. The manure is next shoveled by hand into the furrows ten or so at a time, with the tractor being moved three or four times before turning around at the end of the rows and entering the next set of ten or fifteen rows. A half-acre field, with two of us working, can be manured in less than two hours this way. Once the manure is spread, I unhitch the lift, put on the bedshaper, and run it up and down the furrows, covering and packing in much of the manure below the now shallower rows, where it will lie in a foot-wide band about six inches from the future planting. A second side-dressing of manure will be applied in the same way in mid-spring, using cultivator hiller disks instead of the bedshaper.

Smelly work, yet of the things I do on the farm nothing else feels quite as right as digging manure out of a pen and hauling it and spreading it—both in the rhythmic wide swinging exercise of the work and in the sense of completing and rounding out the biological cycle. And the smell is perhaps the point—because it is an unmistakable sign that something important is going on. Our unrecycling age is fast learning that life becomes difficult unless we allow as large a place to disintegration and decay as to creation and production, and all the other processes by which animal and vegetable matter are broken back down into fodder for the next generation of beings.

Although such thoughts have led me back to using animal manure in recent years, there is little that I can establish with anything resembling scientific precision about the effects of my practices. It is all mostly guess and hunch. It has to do with the look of the land, the feel of the soil, the smell of the landscape, the lushness of growth in the plants I tend, and how they sustain themselves through dry spells and other times of extreme. This feel, these sensations, are what I farm for.

And it pleases me to produce goods that will in fact not last very long: bulbs and flowers and fruits and vegetables that will be eaten, decay and disintegrate, and pass back into the biological cycle, things that will not last forever.

In an age that has littered the planet with permanent

garbage and toxic waste, there is much to be said for basing a
living on crops which by definition submit readily to the
forces of decay, and whose immortality is of another kind,
lying rather in the endless passage through cycles of life and
death.

*

23

HOW TO FARM

BUT FERTILIZER IS part of the larger question, How to Farm?

Every square foot of earth is different. No farmer's experience will be exactly like any other. Much of any farmer's experience is bound to remain deeply private. A result can be Cranky Farmer Talk—such as what follows.

As a farmer you are subject to all kinds of advice and pressure to farm this way or that, according to what is in fashion or what is considered safe or profitable or efficient. The labor of farming isolates the individual farmer more than it brings farmers together, and in isolation the weight of these influences is magnified and distorted.

The synthetic fertilizer and chemical and seed companies tell you that if you do it their way, you'll be productive and profitable. Collectively they house perhaps the greatest economic power of all. Throw in the equipment companies here too, those that make the machines that apply all the powders and potions that feed, kill, ripen, dry out. Plus the college and university research system which helps agribusiness think up new potions and powders and machines to put them on with.

Environmentalists come at you from the opposite direction. No, you can't do that, it'll poison the soil, the water, ruin the biosphere. The strictest environmentalists probably want you to give up farming altogether.

The organic lobby wants you to farm their way, for what they define as the good health of the soil and all eaters of food.

The Soil Conservation Service wants you to keep soil from blowing away and washing into streams and rivers. They also want you to conserve water.

The banks and the Farmers Home Administration want you to farm in a profitable way, no matter what the means, so you can pay back your loans.

Your neighbors would rather whatever you do didn't smell, blow around, make too much noise.

Your fellow farmers, if there are any left, will most likely be running around and looking for the right way to do things and will regard each other's practices as misguided, pointless, expensive, dangerous, too much work, or all five. "I tried that and it didn't work," they'll cheerfully say. Borrowing money may be the only experience they have truly in common.

People who don't farm but who love the idea of other people farming will want you to keep farming no matter what, perhaps so they can talk about farming during the more serious moments of dinner parties, so they can say, "I know this family who actually still farms." You are a feature of their imaginations, their fantasy lives.

Agricultural bureaucrats want you to farm for any reason at all, mainly because if everybody gave up then they would be out of their jobs: your work gives them job security and maintains the value of their fringe benefits and pension plans.

Most of these interests are trying to sell something, make money, make a living. The organic press is in business to print books and magazines, and I doubt their business practices differ much from Exxon or Ortho. The glossy publications of environmental organizations are bound to require the leveling of so many acres of forests per year, and the production of the inks in their colorful pages the degradation of water quality somewhere, first in the printing, second in the eventual disposal.

All this is a weight I often feel pressing in from out there, the momentum of ponderous institutions seeking members, subscribers, converts, customers, clients, laborers, to contribute to the cost of their overhead and help them keep in balance their own gyroscopes of stability and continuity.

And it explains in part my occasional sensitivity to seemingly innocent questions, by those whose quest for the absolutely pure foodstuff has carried them to the tailgate of my pickup at the farmers' markets. The question usually comes in this form:

"Is your produce organic?"

And it is not that I object to a seriously asked question that requests an answer attended to and discussed, where information is exchanged, not buzzwords tossed back and forth. I will give the customer enough information to judge. If the customer doesn't know how to use the information to make a judgment, then that will be the customer's problem— and of course the customer is always free to seek elsewhere for simplistic answers.

So you ask: "Is your garlic organic?"

Please note. We're standing in the middle of an asphalt desert surrounded by parked cars and pickups. We're in the middle of a city like most that some time ago zoned out barnyards and chicken pens and manure piles supposedly in the interests of health and sanitation, and otherwise made it difficult for people to raise livestock and farm, a city like most that is unable to dispose of its own treated sewage waste in an ecologically sound manner, that has chosen to ignore the more serious dangers of the automobile, plus the problems of all those manufactured products householders are allowed to spray on their yards to kill weeds and bugs.

When I was a kid, tasting the landscape on the way to and from school was how my friends and I got to know it. There was anise growing by the side of the road, whose dry stalks we peeled open in the winter for their chewy white pulp. There were the bittersweet stalks of the yellow clover flowers we sucked on. We sipped nectar out of nasturtiums. We smelled the pepper tree berries, the lantana leaves and flowers. We broke in half the succulent iceplant leaves and smeared them on our hands. We foraged oranges and limes and loquats and mandarins and eugenia berries from orchards and hedges along the road.

On a recent walk along those same curving streets, wondering how many gallons of herbicide and pesticides have been applied to the neat yards one sees so rarely tended by anyone, I knew I should no longer taste this landscape as I walked—not because I was older and more fastidious, but because I feared it had been rendered poisonous over the years.

"Is your stuff organic?"

There will be a moment of hesitation. I will look you in the eye to assess what kind of response you want. If a rhetorical one, I'll say merely: "We have never used any chemical herbicides or pesticides and never will."

Often that suffices. But sometimes I'll see genuine curiosity. Then I'll go on to explain that the only "organic" pesticides I have used are rotenone for bean beetles and sabadilla dust on summer squash, and only occasionally. Yet even these, because they are still poisons, however "organic," I'm still reluctant to handle for a narrowly personal reason, that of my own health. There are of course always some annoying exceptions to my rules, such as fungicides that are unpredictably applied to certain seeds from a company I regularly order from and which I often discover too late to reorder elsewhere. Under many current organic regulations, such seed treatments remain acceptable. And I would argue, if with little confidence, that the quantities of these chemicals deposited in the soil are probably much less than the pollutants distributed into the atmosphere by one short drive in a car—though I know I should find no excuses for my own pollutings in those of others.

I would go on to explain my experience with cottonseed meal and sewage sludge and synthetic fertilizers and how I have dealt with animal manures, and how I hope that the fields and woods and orchards under my care consume enough carbon dioxide and produce enough oxygen to balance partially at least the carbon dioxide I generate with my tractor, my vehicles, fireplace, propane heaters, plus all that's produced in the industrial processes that provide me with electricity and a vast range of manufactured goods and products.

"So what about you?" I would conclude. "What about your life? Is it organically lived?" Here I might pause to summon up the courage to bring up the forbidden subject. "And if I may ask, what about the money you would offer to pay me with? Is it organically earned? In short, how have you managed to solve these problems in your life? Have you actually figured out how to live a clean life in a dirty age?"

Then I will listen. I may hear the rationalizations of a fanatic, fretting over notions of exalted states of bodily purity.

And for good reason. Perhaps in the poisonous desert of a city there is little else you can do besides seek out what you hope is "pure" food. Yet I hope I will also hear the deliberations of someone who understands the endless dilemmas of living in these times, someone who understands the term organic as pointing toward an ideal of how a community might better elaborate itself around the use of its land and water. How it might regard the rural landscapes that surround it, the cycles of nature and the interactions of the vegetative, the animal, the human and the cultural. How it might seek to draw back into its life what the fashion of the moment has exiled to "the country."

The question is posed. I will ask it or not, you will answer it or not. But whether spoken or not, all this and more comes to bear on that instant of suspicion or of trust in which I hand over at last a small sack of garlic in exchange for a few pieces of paper.

These will be new and crisp or wrinkled and smudged. Either way, as always, they will be engraved with magical images and words, and will reveal nothing about the uses to which they have been put.

But enough. Thank you. It's been good talking to you. Enjoy your garlic.

End of Cranky Farmer Talk.

24

HOEING

IN ANOTHER TEN YEARS or so perhaps I'll be so good with the tractor that I won't need to go over my garlic fields by hand at all.

The prospect pleases me. It is what I will work toward. Yet I will also miss the company of my fields, whose most interesting news can only be obtained by spending hour after hour in them with a hoe.

The purpose of early cultivation is to aerate the soil, to eliminate competition from weeds, to mix in and cover fertilizer. When the garlic is small and not yet fully rooted, tractor cultivation will be most effective. With cutters and knives and sweeps and hillers and shields set just right (though I find it rare that I manage to do everything just right), you can in theory either bury most weeds or cut their roots, even those growing right next to the garlic—supposing your stand is of an unusually uniform height. Often it is not, and then you have to decide whether the plants you'll damage are worth the time you'll save not cultivating by hand. If there's anyone around to pay you for the time thus saved.

Even though machinery is involved, there's bound to

be something idiosyncratic about how this is done—which you can discover by wandering through any agricultural equipment salvage yard whose heaps of scrap iron form a disorderly compendium of all those different ways farmers have moved earth around. Every couple of years I have driven out to Rocky Ford, Colorado, and picked through as many of its four or five used-farm-equipment yards as I had time for in a day, the largest of which spreads out over forty acres. Each time I have come back with something to improve my cultivator. One year it was depth-gauge wheels, to keep the cutting blades at a uniform height. Another year it was a large colter disk that rolls slicing through the earth, to keep the cultivator tracking in a straight line like a keel. Then it was a set of hiller disks, to heap dirt up against the plants. Then a set of shields, to prevent the dirt being heaped up by the hillers from dumping on top of the plants. Plus the assorted clamps and bars to bolt all these things together. Plus, over the years, two types of planters, several toolbars, vegetable knives and sweeps of varying widths and lengths, furrowing and refurrowing shovels, and the things I have picked up thinking they might be useful but which I haven't yet found a use for.

My two-row cultivator now consists of exactly a dozen such wheels, blades, hoods, and points that all have to be adjusted vertically and laterally to run through my garlic rows without disturbing the roots, without knocking over or burying the plants, without slicing them off, yet while cutting or burying as many weeds as possible, while straddling a two-row bed some forty-five inches wide at a speed of three to five miles an hour—and while I try to manage the neat trick of steering the tractor in a straight line ahead at the same time as I'm sitting twisted around in the seat, head turned back, noting the action of the dark wakes of soil washing up against the twin rows of plants.

Men are too much fascinated by machines, and women too little, for there not to be a strong sexual aspect to them. The connection was first inadvertently made for me by my father, who kept an old pinup calendar in the garage at the end of his workbench. It was tacked on a wall between the grinder and the drill press, amid oil cans and drawers of nuts and bolts and electrical and plumbing fixtures, a shrine of sorts surrounded by greasy offerings. Crouching with hands on hips and smiling, and mounted on a piece of cardboard held to the wall by a nail, the scantily clad pinup could be swung back to reveal the peach-colored flanks and breasts and flushed cheeks of a reclining nude. I would have been tall enough at five or six to reach up over the workbench to flip back the cover image.

And later, but well before I knew anything more about sex than the little revealed by the flashing calendar, I dreamed of phallic pistons and vaginal combustion chambers and the ecstasies of internal combustion engines, and all those explosions and hissings and clickings, and the neat trick by which reciprocal motion is translated into the rotary, and thereby into the linear, mimicking the action of limbs and joints.

At puberty I bought from a friend the bodiless chassis and engine block of a Model T Ford, which I fretted over in the backyard until I sold the pieces back at a slight loss a year later. The only thing I managed to do was paint the engine block. Pistons and crankshaft and camshaft and valves stayed in their wooden box except for occasional examinations of a mildly pornographic nature. I learned nothing or much, depending on the point of view. My father, who probably never wanted to see another Model T, no doubt thought the episode a failure—yet I discovered in all those moonings over the wheeled skeletal form, which sat on the site of my former sandpile, that machines are never just machines but are also the incarnations of an extravagant dream-life. There would always have to be some roaring or humming or buzzing metallic thing, some male-invented machine, at the center of everything I did, which I later came to see as a curse. The dream-life of tractors is no different from cars, only perhaps more private, and the apparently useful work of these machines lends their fantasists an air of innocence.

Such power is best used sparingly, even reluctantly. Running a tractor with a cultivator up and down the close-set rows of garlic always seems an anxious business, and I find it can be done only once or twice in April and early May. Later than that, when the garlic is more nearly mature and when I'm concerned about disturbing the fully rooted plant, tractor cultivation involves yet more risks—of cutting too deeply or running over plants or even pulling up plants or of compacting the soil. Late in spring, weeds will be less a matter of competition than a hindrance to the imminent operations of harvesting. You can always let them go, the lamb's-quarters and tumbleweeds and ragweed and oats and wild sunflower and all the rest—but at a certain price, because they will later plague you by fouling the tractor undercarriage or toolbar or by poking you in the eye or dropping stickery seeds down your neck as you bend over to pull the garlic, or by concealing more than a few bulbs in the rampant growth that can take place in mid-June just before harvest.

So, toward the end, not long before harvest, I go back to the hoe and the file, but now in the heat and humidity, under a hat, and with the difficult knowledge that the only way to do it is one chop and one step and one row at a time. Now is when I get to know the condition of my

soil foot by foot, from the high and low ends of the rows
where the ground is packed hard from irrigation water
standing too long, and through the occasional rocky stretches
in between, and those patches of desert where ants or
gophers have been busy. I hoe through the morning,
working away from the shade of the trees and then back
toward it, where I have shed a jacket and where the water
jug waits, and an apple or two in a paper sack. "I'll do ten
rows today" or "I'll do twenty" or "I'll finish the field," I tell
myself, working at first against the early morning bottomland
pooling of cold air and then against the rising heat, with
breezes curling through loosened clothing and leaves
brushing up against ankles and calves, and nails clogging with
dirt, and the desiccating juices of grasses and weeds stiffening
and cracking the skin of fingers, rendering hands rough and
sensitive at the same time; and knees and back and shoulders
complaining more loudly with each swooping bend.

Hoeing: that activity in which two sides of your
being war with each other and without which perhaps the
work would never get done, the side that notes the easeful
passage of cars and trucks and motorcycles on the road
nearby and the flight of planes overhead, and that thinks of
all the other things he could be doing other than this.

The disgrace of it all, my ego once raged, the
humiliation and pain of being held to the torture of hoeing.
Hoeing breeds envy at the world that does not need to hoe,
at the grace of the fisherman's cast, or the adrenaline rush of
the hunter, or the languor of those who gather nuts and
berries and mushrooms from the wild, at friends whose hands
will never be cracked or stained brown and green or be
coated in that chapped roughness that makes all touch an
irritation, at cheerful hikers who climb mountains and camp
beside streams and lakes—at all those who merely walk the

ground and who do not crawl it as if it were vertical, a cliff to be scaled weed by weed, chop by chop. Why do this? Why bother? Why inflict this upon your body?

Yet I listen much less to this voice, the voice of ease, which would arrange for the world to feed it and dress and groom and house it with the least amount of its own labor of any kind, and which has led me too many times into rage at the injustice of it all—as if this voice is interested in justice. No, it seeks advantage. And knows it.

And so the oddly contented mutterings of another voice have become more and more audible, that patient fellow who points out the beneficial effects of exercise and who suggests that the responsibilities of social living dictate the need to haul water and cut wood and hoe your rows. Who knows that there can be no metaphor here, unless eating and clothing and housing oneself, unless consumption itself, are to be somehow transformed into metaphors too.

And who knows that there can even arise a sense of almost erotic pleasure at learning to move the body well again, even in a task the envious self will call demeaning: a pleasure in the well-placed blade that slices through the stalk with a slight hesitation and pull, at the bending down and standing up with a dance-like grace, at attending the workings of one's own hands and arms and feet and legs, at taking even a certain pride at their weathered and work-scarred forms. And who can gradually claim the right to point to all accumulations of small gestures over the days and months and years that bloom into something as quietly satisfying as a field of garlic or a mud house or a small farm, and all that which has been labored for, not simply bought or found or taken.

This voice dimly knows something about the nature of time itself. It can assume an attitude of benign indifference to everything, even those rows of plants I am straddling in the heat and working through with my hoe. It knows, this voice, why it's pointless to question the search for lamb's-quarters or sunflower or oats growing right beside the white and green striated stalks of my plantings, it knows simply that they must be pulled again and again.

It observes from deep within this labor. If briefly, if dimly, it can grant relief from the human scheme, from systems of status based on envy and anxiety, and their haunting yet banal images that can crowd against that which the eye could actually observe. It is blind and deaf to the representations and symbols that carry power in that other world and is open at last to that which pours into the senses as the smell of garlic and as the scent of the earth being worked, the perspiring presence of that laboring beast with nudging testicles, and the sounds of hoe creaking and scuffling and dinging, and of breathing and the creak of joints, pad of footsteps, rustle of leaves—as flooded now toward noon with a light I will soon seek shade from indoors, in the refuge of a cool breeze through an open window in earthen walls.

Am I free?

I gather up jacket, water jug, file. I go home, wearily fitting myself into the pickup for the short drive, my whole being funneling toward food and rest, in a kind of plummeting fall back toward the social world. It will restore itself as I plunge, and will embrace me in possessions and comforts.

Am I free? I step inside the earthen walls of the living room. A cool breeze will be blowing through the west windows. Someone will have brought in the bright harvest of junk mail. I will cast a glance at the little pictures, the images and icons by which we stimulate and frighten each other in the darkness of our shelters. How odd, this power.

[133]

Later, dozing off, I will think that perhaps it is all more complex than that, perhaps even incomprehensible.

But for the moment at least, no matter. After a morning of hoeing, you can rest, and push away all the other claims, and inhabit for a time another world, and dream of only leaves and roots and earth.

✳

25

COMPANIONS

I'M ALWAYS SURPRISED at how well I know them.

You think you forget certain things or that you don't
pay much attention to them—somehow they enter your
consciousness as images without names—until there, in the
hot sun, bending over, you become conscious of your fingers
working away to find the main stem of a wild morning glory
that would crowd out the lettuce or tomatoes, basil or statice.
The vines snag on the hoe and pull it off course, dangerously
close to plants you would be rescuing; you reach down and
tug at the vine and work your fingers toward where it roots,
often right next to another plant. The fingers know this work.
The mind need say nothing to them.

There is bindweed, a clever vine with a rich
subterranean life, which has established patches here and there
in most of my fields, seed and root carried by the cultivator or
tiller or some other means. Its white trumpet flowers tinged
with salmon pink could be seen as beautiful by someone
ignorant of the plant's habits. In the semi-wild of our man-
made margins it will occupy the verges of roads and highways
and claim the bounty of drainage off the pavement that flows
its way—and where it hopes to hitch a ride to a new location.

With water and fertilizer it will grow into bunched tangles of lush vegetation made up of innumerable fine-stemmed runners and long folded leaves of dark green that will bind up whatever you have planted there. If left to grow rampant, hoe and even rototiller can be defeated, unless you first pull the bunches up by hand and carry them out of the field and then work at chopping back the new shoots. Unlike morning glory with its single vulnerable tap root, bindweed's mass of shoots are all viable even when chopped up. Bindweed can be crowded out by plantings of grass, and eradicated by two or three years of frequent tillage, but these are not possibilities in our courtyard out the front door where it has established itself among the paving stones, redoubt from which it launches forays under the door sill and the foundation itself, popping up through the adobe floor to climb up lamp and telephone cords to peek into my wastebasket and filing cabinet and up over the edge of my desk. There is nothing I'm willing to use beyond my own hands to eradicate it; fortunately the stands in my fields are kept in place by tillage and green manure crops and are not yet expanding at an alarming rate.

Lamb's-quarters—or locally: quelites—are edible when small as a "spinach" raw in salads or lightly sautéed. The undersides of their fleshy spade-shaped leaves are tinged with purple during the edible stages, up to a foot in height. Left untended they'll grow to four or five feet, anchored by a deep taproot that makes them almost impossible to pull up except in wet ground. The tiny seedlings hide out in the garlic rows in such a way that a few plants always manage to escape my cultivation and even survive the chisel plowing and general trampling of the harvest day, to stand bent and limp in the dusty, dry field, and sometimes they will even outlive the shallow furrowings with which I cover the buckwheat seed a week or so later. Quelites are related to quinoa, cultivated by the Incas for the grain and now being coaxed into cultivation in North America. I judge from the size of the plant whether the end of a row, or an edge row, has slipped out of control and is to be abandoned the rest of the season. The tall, branched plants reach out and claim territory on the horizontal, and their tough and fibrous stalks cannot be readily chopped up by a hand tiller. Only the tractor mounted tiller or the mower-mulcher will be a match for them where there is room for the equipment to work. In narrow spaces I have resorted to long-handled pruning shears to cut them back.

Their upward branching habit and mature toughness is akin to ragweed, which will grow in open fields like quelites but seems to prefer the company of buildings, eaves, the dripline of trees and shrubs, and borders of paths and roads. There it will bound into growth at the lightest rain, having kept a low profile until then; its deep taproot makes it impossible to pull up in the often-hard ground it can thrive in, and at its four- and five-foot maturity nothing less than a sharpened shovel or pruning shears can whack it down—to showers of fine yellowish pollen.

Besides quelites other edible weeds—elsewhere crops—inhabit my fields. Pigweed or amaranth starts out with innumerable tiny seedlings that appear insignificant for a time. It is hard to get them all out with hoe or fingers, and like quelites they don't mind some shade during their start in life, which my plantings conveniently provide. Pigweed is more succulent, or succulent longer than quelites, which means it's easier to weed out later in the season, though eventually its pinkish stalk will also toughen in order to support a thick and prickly seed head of hundreds of tiny seeds which juncos and sparrows will pick out in the winter as it stands above the snow. Its grain, like quinoa, is moving back into fashion.

Verdulaga or purslane favors my coolest field. It can be used as a salad green or sautéed like quelites. It's a low-lying, spreading succulent with waxy teardrop leaves branching off a single taproot. As a weed—by which I mean a plant that gets in the way of my intentions—it does not much interfere with my work. Also, when mature, it suffers an insect parasite that often completely eradicates it in mid-summer.

Then there's Russian thistle or tumbleweed, which I think of more as a spring than summer weed, but there's always the odd plant that sneaks through, and the spidery seedling—said to be edible—slowly expands into a flattened round ball, taproot cleverly protected by prickly branches. It is a weed for all seasons, one that waits for winter and then spring again, for the winds to pull it free of its moorings so that it can set off on its bounding travels across fields and roads and into rivers and ditches, scattering seeds on the way. Beached, it looks like a kind of sea-creature, or the husk of one, like a giant urchin.

There are others. Two of our fields are bottomland, and one of them, on the south side of the river, is sandy and rocky and more open and desert-like. On its edges grow cholla cactus and chamisa, in whose spindly branches ladybugs lay eggs, and these drought-loving plants would readily reclaim the field were I to withdraw. I tried only once to grow garlic there and discovered that the soil could not hold the moisture long enough for the shallow-rooted plant. The two-acre field now serves for squash, gourds, pumpkins, and some seventy peach, apricot, and apple trees.

Its sandy, rocky earth specializes in burred and barbed weeds. From August on, it's perilous to walk over there in anything except boots. Parts of the orchard are infested with two types of grassy burrs which cling to cuffs and shoelaces and gloves and which must be gingerly picked off. The spines sting—a useful message that tells you not to eat them but which also seems self-defeating: Were you not prodded by painful stings around ankles and wrists you would well transport the burrs a considerable distance, thus enlarging their territory.

The champion here is the goathead or cabrito, an attractive low-lying plant with fine leaves and a tiny bright yellow flower that produces a seed head barbed with three points, each tipped with a stinging substance that has almost as much staying power as the bite of a red ant. Cabritos looked forward to the advent of the rubber tire and have no doubt caused the invention of various devices to prevent or repair punctures in bicycle tires. They don't cling to vertical surfaces as well as burrs, favoring instead the flat and horizontal; and on our treads and artificial soles they distribute themselves down the middle of our paths and tracks. I can't imagine what softly soled Native Americans did about cabritos in ancient times, except avoid areas where they grew rampant. I doubt I will ever be able to eradicate the weed from the rocky soil of the field across the river where it thrives, unless I convert all the land to grass and trees; in the meantime, I watch where I step when in sandals and where I reach bare fingers to weed early in the summer, and work in leather gloves and boots later on. Fortunately the plant prefers dry, sandy ground to rich cultivated soil, and I find it easy to keep the verges of our bottomland fields more or less clear with an occasional swipe of a shovel blade.

These are the summer weeds I have come to know best over the years. They mark the progress of the growing season as well as my intentional crops, to the point that I probably could not imagine my fields without them anymore, these rivals for light and water and fertilizer. But the game is never over. In August and early September weeds with yellow daisy-like flowers and blue-green foliage suddenly shoot up in the fields, and their branching leaves can soon claim enough light to slow the lower competition. They mirror the wild sunflower in their bloom, but sunflower with its broad leaves and rapid growth is easily weeded out of the early summer field; few will survive my cultivations except at the wet edges of the fields. No, these others whose name I don't know come late, as if knowing by then that I will be turning my attention elsewhere and that I'll be willing to let them get away with their last-minute claim. Often they'll be right, particularly in a season that comes to a quick, abrupt close of an early frost. But in a longer year I know that they'll be in the way, they'll shade, they'll steal moisture and nutrients, they'll be in the way of the last hurried pickings, and if I have my wits about me I'll see that they're hoed out of my fields.

Around this time will appear one of the last weeds of the season, a wild aster. This fine-leaved plant with purple stems and small lavender flowers with yellow centers will mature so late that I think of it as having its own separate little season after all mine are over. It can grow to a height of two feet, providing an uncanny display even after a hard freeze has devastated nearly everything around it.

And then the very last weed of all, whose light green blades tinged with red emerge anytime from mid-August to mid-October: garlic. Not garlic that I have planted but bulbs and bulbils and rounds that were missed or dropped during harvest and which have survived being tilled under with the buckwheat later in the summer, and cloves and seed tops that ended up in the compost heap and then were spread out on a field, garlic that finds itself in the wrong field at the wrong time, or in the wrong place in a field about to be planted in garlic: in short, a weed. Weeds, these plants, but only rarely can I bring myself to hoe them back, though now and then I'll rescue the odd clove or bulb that has surfaced and not yet begun to root.

There it is, crop and weed both; and next year in the fields where it has persisted—as a weed—much of it will be cut and maimed by the tractor cultivator or run over and stepped on during hand work, yet will still survive the harvest to reappear again in the fall amid the statice or the basil or the onions, or whatever other crop I'll be growing in the former garlic patch. The inopportune green shoots, the soon abundant leaves, will mock the later and more timid apparitions of my plantings in straight disciplined rows—as ever calling into question most of my elaborate procedures and thus suggesting that somehow there are better ways still to do most of what I do.

Weeds: perhaps they state the perpetual error of human ways, or a perpetual error in the ways of human thinking. This is why we know them so well, why we're so familiar with them, even as they remain mostly nameless and mostly forgotten in our waking, conscious lives.

*

26

PYROTECHNICS

By MID-MAY garlic will have attained its full growth. Arching flat leaves will shade much of the two-foot space between rows, and the plants will seem able to grow on forever, becoming taller and more abundantly leafy by the day. Some of the leaves will stand a foot and a half high, the ones at the wet end of an irrigation row where silt and fertilizer have deepened the topsoil.

A rich bluish green marks the leaves of top-setting garlic from the paler non-bolting types. I feel drawn toward the oceanic tinge and like to comb through the plants a last time with my hoe, to linger in their presence. Corn and tomato and chile pepper plants exert this same almost animal attraction, for lack of a better term. Out of the corner of my eye I have wondered if in some sense they are aware of my tending presence, particularly in the celebratory abundance of their prime. Other plants I hold to be indifferent—carrots, lettuce, even onions and leeks, plants which keep to themselves and go about their business no matter what—but not the others, though words will fail to pick out the invisible filaments that tie the vegetative presences to that special form of alertness and intelligence we house absently under a sense of personal preference. Fertilized and irrigated and weeded, with the brown earth shaded under the leafy canopy, the May field of top-setting garlic reaches a climax of leaf growth at around that time of spring when surrounding orchards are fully leafed out and beginning their new growth. By the end of the month, beneath the ground, the startlingly white bulbs splotched with purple are nearly done with their own serious business. Within two or three weeks you will notice the faint loss of vigor in the leaf that signals that the plant is turning back in on itself and transferring the last of its leaf-housed energies down into the bulb.

In my late hoeings I now and then dig down with my fingers and examine the size and shape of the bulb. Occasionally I'll pull up a volunteer growing a little to one side of the planted row, one likely to be run over by the tractor during harvest. The aroma of fresh garlic, more herb-like and sharper than the mature bulb, and mixed with the emanations of damp earth, explodes in the nostrils as visitation of the harvest soon to come. These early bulbs, which haven't yet completed the process of dividing into cloves but which are perfectly usable in the kitchen, bruise easily and can spoil by turning bright turquoise green throughout. Later when the cloves are completely differentiated such damage will be confined to the clove affected and not spread; and when fully mature, even a badly damaged clove can remain viable throughout much of the summer. Here, perhaps, an advantage garlic gains by dividing its bulb up into ten to twenty separate compartments of stored energy. A wound will most likely be confined to a clove or two, and a damaged or diseased clove, isolated from its fellows by several layers of skin, will less readily sink the whole bulb, rot the whole barrel. Or even supposing the worst, which is always a man with a shovel or garden fork digging carelessly, slicing right through the middle of the plump bulb—as I have done more times than I wish to remember—then there is still a good chance of at least one-tenth or even one-twentieth of the bulb remaining in the ground, in the form of the solitary clove that escaped disaster. Thus the plant survives even my efforts, with all my steel tools, all my highly mobile protein, all my personal and collective memory. By late September a seemingly well-harvested patch of garlic will tell you quite clearly in the new green points emerging just how many cloves you missed. Usually, I find, it's a lot.

Late spring, at the same time the bulb is completing its underground labors by filling out and dividing into cloves, top-setting plants are preparing to make the flamboyant gesture that distinguishes them from more acculturated and inward-turning cultivars, whose leaf growth has been trained to die back like most onions and leeks without the final flourish of seed stalk and top.

But the structure that top-setting garlic sends up is no ordinary growth, no mere vertical tube of the sort produced by those onions or leeks or elephant garlic plants that are allowed to go to seed. Instead we're presented with a unique kind of performance of the sort I have never seen in any other plant. Its mechanics have fascinated me for years.

What happens is this. Toward late May, from the center of the plant where new leaves emerge by the pair, what appears to be a last single leaf will thrust upward. Its singleness distinguishes it at first. Then there follows a whitish swelling several inches below the point. Then as it grows, the swelling enlarges into a white arrow-shaped pod or spathe, no longer a leaf-tip, as supported by a round stalk or scape, no longer a leaf. Five or six inches out into the world the pod leans to one side, and then the stalk proceeds to grow first into one coil, then into a second, both about an inch in diameter, in the manner of a pig's tail or bed spring. The coiling takes place over the course of a week or two.

The stalk next resumes vertical growth, bearing the coils higher, expanding as they go. The pod grows slowly larger. In time its arrow form will shorten and fill out to become heart-shaped. As the stalk grows taller the coils will gradually disappear, until the seedpod perches atop a two-and-a-half- to three-foot rod.

Whereupon the bumpy white sheath, the spathe, will open and peel back like the cargo-loading end of a transport plane or the instrument housing of a spacecraft to reveal a cluster of plum-colored bulbils that will sway gravidly back and forth in the wind. The construction of this elevator, this pump, this platform, is the work of about a month.

Anyone walking past a field of top-setting garlic in the coiling stage will marvel at what is going on and what it might mean. The white seedpod and the coiling necks make you think of swans or bird-like creatures. This is not the random grasping and reaching out of root or tendril toward diffuse plumes of light and moisture. The seed stalks suggest purposeful movement or exertion as arrested by stop-motion photography. They seem to know what they're doing and where they're going: they have something precise in mind.

Uprightness helps, uprightness is mobility, uprightness is all. A stalk serves as the foundation for the elevated drying platform and then the launching pad that will send the seed out into the world. This much is obvious. Summer is a time when every possible strategy for furthering the throw can be found in any field going to seed. But garlic has a special problem. Bulbils are not seeds. They are tiny bulbs, many of them hundreds of times heavier than the seeds of the grasses that provide the most formidable competition, of the thistles and dandelions and milkweed or cottonwood or cattails that

[145]

all equip their featherweight cargo with parachutes or wings or fluff for soaring and floating, or of those plants whose seeds are provided with barbs for clinging.

The problem lies in holding that much weight in a structurally precarious position high off the ground, and long enough for the cluster of bulbils to dry, seal themselves up, detach themselves from each other, in preparation for their launching. It is a problem that herbaceous plants and builders of radio towers, oil rigs, bridges, and skyscrapers have solved in innumerable ways.

The coils may be part of the solution: they may serve to build a degree of torsion into the stalk, thereby strengthening it and thereby adding to the time it can hold its cargo aloft and thereby increasing its chances of wider distribution through the action of the wind or the neighbors' running dogs or horses or cattle. And of course there will always be that curious human who will pluck off a few seed tops and mill the clusters between thumb and palm, will examine the bulbils, which look like pale pomegranate seeds, and will peel off the pinkish skin and chew on the yellowish-white garlic flesh—it is identical to the bulb—and then cast the rest into the bushes a few feet later or a few miles away.

What is also odd for our earth-hugging plant is this sudden late interest in sun and air, heat and light, in the form of the arm the bulb thrusts up out of the earth at the last minute and with which it hurls bulbils into the wind—or what seems odd in relation to the way we have come to think of garlic. But as I have said, this may be its primary reproductive strategy, which for thousands of years growers have tried to breed out of it in order to curb its profligate reproductive ways.

In any case the growth of the seed stalk is also a signal to begin withholding water in order to stress the plant, which encourages the bulb to enfold itself in tight layers of protective skin. As the time draws near I pull up more and more garlic to check the development of clove differentiations. The weather can always fail to cooperate during the last weeks when you're trying to dry up a field, but the effect of an ill-timed rain will be lessened if the soil is well on the way to drying out beforehand.

Determining the moment of harvest is another problem subject to obsessive study. Harvesting, like planting, is a rough-and-tumble business. If you harvest too early, before the bulbs are fully differentiated, then you risk spoiling much of the crop with injuries a mature bulb could easily tolerate two weeks later. If you wait too long, the skin can darken with various types of black and brown mold, and the bulbs will fall apart as you try to lift them from the ground. Top-setting garlic appears to be more sensitive to these problems than non-bolting types, which hold together better in the earth even if left well beyond the ideal harvest date.

The optimum pulling time for top-setting garlic appears to last no more than about a week. I wait for that moment when the seed stalk is just about to straighten up, when it resembles an upright shepherd's crook, with the seed top dangling upside down from the hook, coils otherwise absorbed into stalk.

At sixty-five hundred feet and a latitude of about thirty-six degrees north, this takes place reliably around the third or fourth week of June from a crop planted the previous fall. In damper parts of the field, at the bottom end of irrigation rows, the plant can still be quite green even if beginning to look less vigorous, leaves and stalks and roots having fed their reserves of energy to both bulb and top sets. And in all, plants will be far from dried out except in those patches where the soil is exceptionally shallow or sandy.

I have been told that if the seedpods are nipped off, the bulb will grow larger, which I have not tested. The bulbs are almost fully formed when the seed stalk begins emerging, so I'm inclined to believe the benefits would be marginal at best. And then there's the matter of the tedious stoop labor of trimming back the stalks of tens of thousands of plants one at a time when there's already too much to do.

As part of the harvesting operation itself we used to walk through the fields and cut off the mature seedpods into buckets with garden shears, leaving the stalk in place, a pleasant task during which everyone became spattered with garlic juice. A few years ago I worked out that this sudden breach in the hydraulic economy of the plant was responsible for the skin sloughing prematurely off the bulb in storage, often leaving the yellowish flesh of the cloves completely exposed. This was unattractive and probably affected the keeping quality of the crop. We now pull the whole plant and cut off the seedpods after the plant is dry on the racks in the shed. Even out of the earth the pods continue to mature, sucking the last moisture and nutrients out of the stalk and thus helping to dry the plant in a gradual manner. To handle the two- and three-foot-tall plants with bulbs on one end and pods on the other requires care to keep pods in particular from tangling, but it can be managed with practice.

Our three or four garlic fields do not all mature at once. Slope in relation to the angle of the sun or the shade of nearby trees and soil depth and planting date all seem to bear on when a patch finally matures. Fields planted in top sets a year and a half previously will be ready to pull before any of the fields planted in cloves nine months before, and non-bolting types will be ready first of all.

The exact date is never quite predictable. Hot dry weather in late spring can accelerate the ripening stages, just as heavy rains can slow them. And though I'm much less anxious than I used to be about these last weeks before harvest, I find it best to stay around the place and settle my brooding self to watch for the arrival of that moment I set in motion nearly a year before. Now my work is to haunt the fields and walk through them and pull the odd garlic in search of those signs—the straightening neck, a faint yellowing in the leaves—that tell me that the long incubation in earth can at last come to an end.

*

27

A HISTORY OF
DIGGING

PULLING THINGS OUT of the ground is never as easy as you would like to imagine.

Bend over and reach down and grab a mature garlic plant by the stalk and pull. A sharp snapping sound will announce that you have broken the neck, that the lizard has left its tail, the fish has got away, and better luck next time. Only if the soil is unusually loose to a depth of eight to ten inches will you have some hope of coaxing your garlic bulb to the surface by tugging on its fragile neck.

The sand and clay loam I farm in is strong enough to make an adobe brick that will last centuries if kept dry. Our soil, even when damp, is clingy, heavy stuff. And though garlic roots less elaborately than many plants, a mophead of thick white roots can secure the plant so well that it's rare you can pull up a bulb without breaking its neck or pulling it from the roots, thereby tearing off the germinating end of many of the cloves. Fully mature, going into the hiding of summer dormancy, the bulb will let its roots die back and also its stalk; and if you leave the plant too long in the field you're likely to find yourself pulling up nothing more than a handful of dry leaves and stalks, even from fairly loose soil. A garlic bulb plus roots is anchor, ballast, storage tank combined: it anchors the long stalk atop which waves the launching pad of bulbils, hope against hope, while banking its accumulated capital against the future underground, out of sight, out of harm's way. I'm embarrassed to say that it took me nearly fifteen years to find a satisfactory method to pry, dig, lift our bulbs out of the ground—and there's still much room for improvement.

Most fruits and vegetables reach some distinct ripening point when it's clear they're ready to be picked, a weakness or brittleness at the stem or a dying back of the roots that almost seems to encourage the final plucking or pulling. This often corresponds to that moment when the parent plant dies back, having stowed the future in its seemingly lifeless seeds.

In the biological world the only true death is extinction. Egg, seed, spore, nut, root, and bulb are carriers of all our immortalities from generation to generation in parcels large and small. The garlic bulb passes through a continuous metamorphosis from bulb to plant to bulb again with much less dying back than most creatures. Each garlic bulb by weight is between one-tenth and one-fifteenth ancient history. This may be the utility of its antiseptic sulfur-based compounds, to convey such a large amount of seed matter from generation to generation. The garlic clove you slice into your salad dressing has managed to stay continuously alive for tens of thousands of years, immune from the churning biological recycling that takes place in the soil all around it— until that unlucky moment when your knife cuts into its flesh, and you begin feeding your hopes for immortality on its own proven success. By comparison to a garlic clove, how small is the bridge of sperm and ovum across which we pass from one generation to the next. And though garlic has found humankind somewhat useful as an extension of its cloning method of reproduction, and as its global planter and distributor, its agent and guardian of territorial expansion, the bulb can also do without us in a pinch, even at this late date. Hence—perhaps—its stubbornness about coming up out of the ground, its refusal to cooperate at all in its harvest.

Our first sizable patch of top-setting garlic was an eighth of an acre of heavy clay loam, a rich soil that had served for a few years before as our vegetable garden. In order to dig up garlic with a shovel or garden fork in such soil, we had to work in soft ground, which is to say that it had to be wet—and therefore muddy. Even so, we had to pull the plants when fairly green in order to extract the bulbs in one piece.

Our first harvest was conducted without the benefit of mechanization of any kind. We summoned all our friends and issued them short-handled garden forks and various types of shovels, and then we divided ourselves up into groups of diggers and pullers. When the garlic was dug we carried it up to the driveway turnaround and washed the muddy bulbs in laundry tubs and laid them out on the driveway to dry.

There were obvious problems to the method. Digging and pulling were hard on backs and hands. Garden forks bent and broke, even in the damp earth. Carrying the plants heavy with mud up out of the garden tired us all, men, women, children. You can ask friends to help you with this kind of work once or twice, but no more than that.

I solved the carrying problem first. For a hundred dollars I bought a rear-mounted forklift for the tractor. Then I built a half-dozen harvest racks out of wood and chicken wire. These were about six feet wide, two feet deep, three feet tall, and open on the top and back. Each one would hold some three to five hundred pounds of garlic, stacked with the bulbs pressed up against the wire mesh of the long side closest to the tractor, with stalks and seed tops dangling out the open end. With a rack on the tractor no one would have to lug armloads of garlic very far anymore, and we soon learned to encourage people to carry only small bunches in order to avoid bending and tangling stalks. Also, garlic bunches neatly stacked on the harvest racks are easier to unload later.

Next, digging. The first tractor-powered digger was fabricated by Tom Seibel, my singing farmer neighbor and early agricultural mentor; it consisted of a flat steel blade a foot or so wide that I hoped would ride below the bulbs and cut their roots and loosen the earth. From what I later saw in the way of bed-lifter design, we were on the right track. But it didn't work. The blade was too fat to dig its way into the ground most of the time—and if I did manage to seat it in the correct position, rare in many attempts, the tractor proved unable to pull it in a straight line.

Next I tried curved vegetable knives set below ground and attached by vertical standards to the horizontal tool bar. Success was sporadic. Where a field was muddy the tractor wouldn't steer in a straight line and where dry the knives would skip out of the earth altogether. Yet, encouragingly, there were often rows of garlic whose roots were properly cut without too many bulbs sliced in half or run over.

Other shapes of cultivating knives and some minor refinements gave me a barely workable arrangement, at least in soil that was just the right degree of dampness, always difficult to achieve in an irrigated field of variable slope and soil type. The long vegetable knives I came to favor were designed for surface cultivation, not digging; their thin blades flexed beneath the surface, giving irregular results. We still had to use garden forks and shovels for patches at the ends of rows.

Things improved slightly when I bought the larger

[153]

tractor. But by then I was beginning to realize that drying up the fields before harvest would give us a tighter bulb. The thirty-horsepower diesel could pull anything in four-wheel-drive. But in the hard dry ground vegetable knives began to crack, steel standards to bend, clamps to pop their bolts.

About the same time I had bought the chisel plow in order to deal with a hardpan problem, which turned out to be imaginary. I had not yet realized its usefulness for cutting roots invading my fields or its garlic-digging potential. It sat leaning, akimbo, rust and fading red paint darkening into the pitted ebony of farm implements that are not receiving their annual burnishing in the soil, their oilings and greasings, the press of sweaty hands, that are sinking slowly into the earth: there it sat until Tom Seibel suggested I try it for digging garlic.

A single-point chisel plow would serve well to anchor a small yacht. Its point or shoe, a couple of inches wide and eight inches long, rides horizontally eighteen inches below the surface on a broad beveled half-inch thick shank bolted to a three-point hitch; it rides behind the tractor like a stinger until dropped into the ground. I had no doubt come across many chisel plows in my salvage yard explorations and had probably wondered at the desperate conditions that would cause such a thing to be invented.

It is a vast improvement over everything else I have tried but is yet not the perfect implement for digging garlic. My history of digging is not yet complete. Literature for imported root crop bed lifters which work by sawing horizontally through the earth remains in my files, along with forbidding price lists. Another system, much cheaper, uses horizontal disks spinning on bearings to undercut garlic and onions, and this is what I'll try next.

In the meantime, toward the end of June I'll continue

to hitch up the chisel plow and set out for the patch or field we'll be pulling a day or two later. I start with a middle row, inserting the tractor tires into the narrow irrigation furrows between the tall plants, and then drop the point in between the two rows the wheels straddle. Within a few feet it sinks deep and takes hold and begins shattering the dry earth below to a radius of a foot and a half or so. And though deep, the point and shank are so far from any bulb that none are cut or bruised. On the surface there's little more sign of the plow's action than a neat zipper-like groove down the row and cracks radiating away from it. As the machine passes over the two- and three-foot high seed tops, the stalks bend over and then stay leaning in the loosened earth around the bulbs. At the end of each row, I'll get down off the tractor and free any garlic plants whose pods have snagged on the hitch or somewhere on the plow, and rescue others that have been pulled out and left in the next row I'll be driving up.

The field is cut. It looks as if a high wind has swept across, bending all the plants over. Within an hour or so, roots snapped by the subsoiling upheavals, weeds will wilt in the high sun and garlic leaves will begin to droop and fade.

The field is cut: yellowing, the plants look suddenly forlorn, abandoned. Below the earth the moist outer skin of the white bulb begins to dry and become glossy and papery in order to seal the bulb, in order to prepare it for its sojourn in the air, the outer space into which it will soon be tugged, pulled, dragged.

*

28

GARLIC PULLS AND
GARLIC WASHINGS

OUR BEST HARVEST in recent years has been nearly eighteen racks. A rack is about six feet long, two wide, three high. It can hold five to six hundred pounds. Of that, half the weight will be in stalks and seed tops, half in garlic bulbs; eighteen racks will therefore yield somewhere between four and five thousand pounds.

Our worst harvest was twelve racks, between two and three thousand pounds, in 1989, a year in which I thought I had at last done everything right. Perhaps I had. But it turned out to be the driest spring and summer in ten years.

These yields are small compared to the commercial fields of central California, where eighteen thousand pounds an acre is not unheard of—presumably with the help of vast quantities of synthetic fertilizers, pesticides, and herbicides, and with little regard for what's happening at the bottom of the field or to the ground water or downstream or to the neighborhood in general.

From the beginning, with our first plot of an eighth of an acre, we knew we needed help. When we got to half an acre, we needed more help. When we reached an acre, we didn't know which was the more overwhelming, the sheer quantity of garlic or the number of friends we had to call on to give us a hand. We were still pulling then, still digging, still working in the wet earth with hand tools and without any kind of mechanical assistance in loosening the earth. And I was still laboring under the ethic of self-sufficiency, which stated that you did it all yourself, with the help of your friends, not with paid labor. I was much possessed by the subtle arrogance of one who expects everyone to rally to his fanatical projects.

First we drafted friends who lived within a radius of a couple of miles, people like us who had moved to northern New Mexico in the late sixties or early seventies to get away from it all, to go back to the land. For their help, we gave them lunch and let them carry away armloads of garlic.

Then as the novelty wore off for our nearby rural friends, we began drafting city friends from Taos and Santa Fe. Eventually we reached as far as Albuquerque, a hundred miles away.

But the farther we had to call for volunteer pullers, the longer it took them to get here, the later they arrived in the morning, and the less time they worked in the field, and the more eating and drinking they tended to do in the house. It was all too seductive. There was the cold beer, the roast chicken, the sliced ham, stuffed grape leaves, the homemade loaves of whole wheat and French bread, the potato salad, the tossed green salad made from our own lettuce and spinach, the desserts, the iced tea, the coffee, and then there was the peace and contentment that follows upon heavy eating occasioned by modest labor.

Laying in provisions for the harvests was costing us hundreds. At the peak we sponsored four gourmet harvest festivals each July. For Rose Mary, who rarely left the kitchen, the harvest became a rumor, not something she experienced except as a caterer. All the while I bounced around on the tractor, hoping everyone was doing everything right. But how could they know? Most of our faraway friends had never pulled garlic before. One young woman, friend of a friend, showed up in fancy leather boots and excitedly announced that this was the first time she had ever stood in a field.

During the gourmet harvest years, we pulled in the morning and washed in the afternoon. I would bring the racks back from the field on the forklift and park them in the driveway turnaround between the shed and the house. Then I would hose them down and move them over one by one to a long washing trough that was fed by an inch and a half pipe down from the acequia. The trough was made out of sheets of corrugated tin wired onto poles and held up by sawhorses. It resembled the placer operation of a primitive gold mine. Three or four people would stand at the trough and scrub mud out of the garlic roots and wash off the leaves and stalks. Someone else would feed them bundles of dirty garlic lifted off the rack. Another would spread out the washed garlic to dry on the driveway, shingling the rows in such a way as to cover the bulbs from the sun.

Hosing down and washing and spreading often went on until the sun lowered and the water became too cold to work in. Then our helpers would hose and dry themselves off, pack up their armloads of garlic and drive back to town.

But the washing went on the next day and the day after and beyond. Often I did most of it. Rose Mary would come out and help for a while. Occasionally a neighbor would drop by and lend a hand.

Hose down. Wash. Spread out. Scoop up, stack in the shed. This is how a ton or two of anything multiplies itself into ten tons of lifting. I felt rich presiding over the racks and rows and stacks of white and purple bulbs and could adapt myself to the meditative labor, which did much to erase memories of the increasingly chaotic harvest mornings.

I would work through the limpid days of late June and early July when the last drifting tufts of cottonwood pollen give body and dimension to the transparency of the air and when the leaves of the trees are still a clear bright green. Each morning the sun would rise into a brilliant blue sky, and a cool breeze scented with wood smoke and pine would roll down from the mountains. The mornings would heat up fast and by noon they took on the character of the high desert that lay to the south, with the pungent chemistry of water splashing on hot dust. Early afternoons thunderheads would unfurl from west to east to gather overhead and shut out the sun; the skies would rumble, a few drops might fall, then clouds part again.

My endless daily zigzag course carried me barefoot squishing through mud near the trough and then across the gritty driveway and in and out of the powdery earth of the shed, to the cool north cement wall, deep within the shadow of the ticking tin roof.

Silence bracketed the timeless workday from the moment in the morning I climbed the ditch bank and got down on my hands and knees and pulled out an old sock that plugged the pipe. A moment later water would gush out on the tin trough thirty feet below and then resound over the edge into a washtub. The splashings sang all day until I climbed back up in the early evening and stuffed the sock back into the pipe, and the sound ceased and then there were only tinkling drips for a moment, then silence.

Thus I observed the days swell and fade from my post at the trough and its ribbons of bright water and bunches and rows of white bulbs streaked with purple.

29

PLAYS, INSTRUCTIONS, HARVESTS

BUT WASHING AND then drying were slowing down the harvest. Bulbs were standing in the ground too long waiting for racks to be emptied and space cleared in the shed. Much as I enjoyed spending days washing garlic I couldn't wash fast enough to keep ahead of the harvest schedule.

And I was concerned that the washing might be sending the wrong signal to the bulb, which should be No More Water, not There's Plenty More to Come.

In order to reduce the number of bulbs with moldy or splitting skin we began to pull from slightly drier ground. When you wet dirt and then dry it suddenly, it turns into adobe lumps, pellets, clods, moving toward the condition of being rock, which only water will reverse. When you agitate dry or somewhat dry dirt, it moves toward the opposite condition of becoming sand or dust. Consequently, as we began pulling our garlic from drier ground we discovered that dirt still clinging to roots and bulbs would slough off in the course of further drying, or most of it at least, and that washing was no longer necessary.

At the same time we began giving up our volunteer crews. A generation of neighborhood schoolchildren were coming of age, contemporaries of our own Adam and Kate. The boys in their early teens were beginning to show up to dig out the acequia each spring. Rose Mary had already run most of the valley's kids through a series of musicals she wrote and directed for the local school from kindergarten through sixth grade. Double-cast so that the actors could also watch the play they were in, with sets by a stage designer friend who had taken refuge from Hollywood in the village, and performed to a cumulative audience of thousands, these were productions of an entirely different order than the usual school plays with their agonizing longeurs. Rose Mary had discovered reserves of memory in her child actors that the educational system no longer bothered to tap, and she was able to rewrite her scenes daily to adapt the parts to her players' personalities. The kids could memorize their new lines in a flash.

These young actors, Hispanic and Anglo, who had played the parts of clowns, kings, bears, elves, dogs, gardeners, ditch-diggers, postmasters and shopkeepers, princesses and courtiers, made up our first paid garlic crews. For many, seventh and eighth graders now, it was their first proper if brief job, and they took it very seriously. Work on the ditch didn't quite count. Anybody could do that. All you had to do was show up. But to pull garlic, you had to be invited. We also paid better, well above the minimum wage.

They were frisky crews. Much of the time they teased each other and talked about movies and TV shows and remembered the plays they themselves had acted in not all that long ago—while the adults among the crew stood back and held silent our own immensely spanning memories and listened to the young remembering when they were little, just a year or two before.

Among the group there were always one or two boys who worked fast, who tried to bunch the garlic up into heavy armloads, who needed to prove something, for whom the job was a race or a competition, and whom I would urge to slow down or to keep bunches small or to help out slower neighbors. There were those who had never worked at anything and who had trouble keeping up, their thoughts turned inward to the difficulties of composing back and arms and legs into coordinated movement. There were those who fueled themselves by mocking friends for the way they worked or spoke or dressed or for the little mishaps that always take place during such labor in the way of things that are dropped, tripped over, bumped into. There were those who had learned to talk to adults but not to their peers, and those who studiously ignored the adults, including their boss—or those who were solicitous of the every gesture of a father suddenly present at last to bestow the gift of commands and orders.

At their age, my first job had been outdoors like this. But alone in the heat, hacking at some weeds with a dull hoe in rock-hard ground, hands rapidly blistering, hired by a man in a gray suit who knew no more of these matters than I: that there were weeds which something should be done about and a boy who needed work. I lasted one morning.

Later, during my first year in high school, I was hired as a gardener by a retired army doctor who lived a short bicycle ride down the road. A thin, small man, he was married to a large woman who reminded me of the family cookie jar, and he wore a pith helmet, glasses, and a cantankerous pocket hearing aid that amplified sounds for the benefit of everyone standing nearby. Often the doctor's asthma kept him inside for weeks at a time, and because of his condition he had taken to writing up elaborate instructions for his young gardeners, of which I was perhaps the third or fourth since his retirement. These little sheets of note paper, sometimes as many as ten pages, would be handed through the kitchen door by his

[162]

solemn wife on those days he was confined to his bed—or presented personally on those afternoons he was able to shuffle about not far from the gangly fellow who was trying to make sense of his messy blue scribbles. The doctor particularly favored the locution "repair to," as in: "Upon watering the avocado trees behind the garage, repair to the begonia garden for further instructions at approximately 4:20."

These afternoons made up the full extent of my formal agricultural and horticultural training. I became an expert on his always vaguely diseased Bermuda grass lawn, and on his sickly orange, lemon, and avocado trees out behind the garage. At times the doctor's asthma would keep him indoors for weeks at a time, and I would be asked inside the stucco house with a red tile roof and dark, creaky interior, where the doctor would extract assurances that the begonias and avocados were still alive outside, and that I was fully aware of the gravity with which his plants must be tended.

The end of my apprenticeship came a year earlier than expected when I was offered a scholarship to combine my last year of high school and first year of college at the University of Chicago. Neither the doctor nor his wife was pleased at the thought of me leaving for such a hotbed of un-American activity, but I was generous in my youthful celebrity and forgave them their narrowness and understood their distress at losing a gardener who was punctual, quiet, and now and then hardworking. And I had become fond of the old doctor and his elaborate prescriptions for his fellow sufferers, his always-ailing plants.

The kids who dug the acequia and acted in Rose Mary's plays and then pulled garlic for us have since gone out in the world to real jobs, to college, the Air Force, the Marines, to war. But new waves of neighborhood kids materialize in late June just when we wonder where we'll find our harvest crew. Our brief jobs come at that point in their

[163]

lives when they want to work, but perhaps not much, and when they need a bit of money, but not a lot, and when they want to work with others rather than alone.

We start at eight. It will be a morning in the last week in June. There need be only seven or eight of us now, down from the fifteen to twenty of the old days of digging garlic by hand out of muddy earth. A day or two before I will have run the chisel plow up and down the rows. Three or four empty racks will be lined up alongside the field, plus one on the tractor. In addition to the thirteen- and fourteen-year-olds, there will often be a couple of friends who have called up and asked to join us. We'll fan out and begin pulling at one end of the field, each person working one or two rows. I urge everyone to take their time, keep their bunches small, pile their bunches evenly on the rack. Rose Mary will arrive in the pickup with an ice chest full of refreshments for our ten o'clock break, and will join in the pulling and will help supervise the younger members of the crew. We'll pause briefly a second time at eleven if the day turns hot.

My job is to keep the tractor-mounted rack close to the crew in order to cut down the hiking back and forth. I'll need to move the tractor three or four times up the ten-row swath we're clearing. In between times I pull with the rest of the crew and help those who are lagging behind and scavenge garlic that has been missed, moving along the bucket and shovel we still need for digging up the odd bulb whose roots cling to an enormous clod.

When a rack is full I raise the lift to its highest position and crank the top-link so as to tip the load back toward the tractor. Then I set off in low gear across the field toward the driveway or the road, hoping not too much garlic will slide out the open side of the rack. In the meantime the stronger boys drag or carry an empty rack into position.

To drive to the shed, lower the rack in the shade, slip out the fork lift, will take between five and ten minutes, depending on whether we're harvesting from the field in front of the house or a quarter of a mile down the road at the Richardsons'. There, if the crew is a fast one, I'll often wait until we have filled up all of the four or five racks brought to the field the day before, or even until after the crew is paid off at noon or one.

At the end of the morning the boys dispel all worries that we may have overworked them. They roughhouse in the dirt or run off to the river to swim, while the girls among themselves make more intricate, long-range plans. And while I set about transporting the last garlic racks back to the shed, Rose Mary gathers up the cooler and carts it back to the pickup, where she'll write out the morning's paychecks.

We've been pulling garlic for some fifteen summers. Perhaps two hundred people have helped us, friends we have fed lunch and given garlic, kids we have plied with iced tea and cookies and paid by the hour. They have helped us pull some fifty tons of stalk, seedpod, bulb, and mud from patches of about a half-acre each spotted over two fields of no more than five acres altogether.

Under the hot sun, the field will be bare. The deep chevron tread of tractor tires will map the progress of the pull. There will be scuffled piles of dirt pushed up by the forklift where it was slid beneath a rack. Here and there huddled clumps of sunflower and lamb's-quarters will be wilting. There will be the odd white flag of a garlic seedpod atop a leaning yellow stalk. An empty garlic rack, one too many, will stand at the edge of the field.

Later I may find a green plastic drinking glass stuck in the crook of a nearby apple tree, probably parked there with ice cubes melting, and then forgotten.

[165]

※

30

FORMS OF WEALTH

AN ECONOMIST FRIEND used to chide me for not taking
into account the value of my own labor.

It's true: nowhere in our account sheets does this item
appear. Rose Mary and I give ourselves no salary. In moments
of self-deprecation, I'll say things like: "Our time is probably
worth fifteen cents an hour." We live not on any profit but
on whatever we manage to snatch from the cash flow.

Not long ago I was introduced to the Amish concept
of labor as a product, not an expense. I had always known
that one of the values of subsistence farming was that it gave
everyone work from the very young to the very old. My
parents used to spend much of the summer with us. For my
father in particular our little farm was his past, which he could
relive, recover, perhaps even rehabilitate—or so I would
guess. Up until his eighties he could easily outwork me most
days, and even now at eighty-six he can still put in a long day
on their two- or three-week annual visit, at an altitude six
thousand feet above what he is accustomed to. One useful
thing my mother has been able to do since a stroke blinded
her five years ago, besides drying the dishes, is to break up
garlic for planting; she looks forward to it months in advance.

When the labor is your own, the notion of profit loses some of its attraction, profit being what owners or investors make from the labor of others. Perhaps to profit from your own labors, you must regard yourself as a machine or an object or an other and be willing to calculate the difference between what you must spend in order to live and work and what you earn from your labors, and thus to draw lines between the parts of yourself that labor and those that do not.

But as human beings we resist such narrowness—at least in ourselves—and sink into all kinds of elaborate rationalizations. What is the business value of a marriage? The children? The landscape, the hills and mountains amid which we live? The river? If I thought in strictly business terms, I would have to draw lines to exclude the very values I ultimately work for.

There are several moments throughout the season when I particularly feel that my own labor is not an expense, not a cost, not a wearing out, and one of them is when I stack garlic through the long hot afternoons of early July.

The garlic shed is a rambling pole barn sheathed and roofed in corrugated tin more or less enclosed on three sides, with the south side open facing the driveway. It started out as a storage shed about fifteen feet square. Now it measures forty by forty. A second shed, thirty-six by twelve, was added a couple of years ago along the east fenceline. These house our supplies, tools, some equipment, and in the winter the tractor and one of the pickups.

It is into these spaces that I must fit 120 rows of garlic plants. One hundred twenty rows of growing garlic takes up an acre and a half, some sixty thousand square feet. The sheds offer shelter to about twenty-five hundred square feet. Half of that area is permanently claimed by supplies and equipment.

The trick is to fit the abundant growth of sixty thousand square feet into an area one-fiftieth that size.

We harvest the whole plant. An unhappy top-setting garlic will measure eighteen inches bulb to seedpod. A happy one will extend three feet. Were we to top the bulbs we'd have much less bulk to dry and store. But we sell most of our garlic by bundling it up into decorative bunches and festooning it with strawberry popcorn, spoon gourds, chile peppers, and heads of wheat. We now handle carefully the once-scorned stalks.

When you pull the whole plant, stalks dry out as moisture is taken up at one end by the bulb and at the other by the seed top. By contrast moisture in the flat leaves must mostly evaporate, and these are what will turn black with mold if the garlic is left in the harvest rack more than a few days or if stacked too-damp in the shed.

Some years ago I devised a system of temporary drying racks made up of short two-by-four sleepers and long one-by-four rails. The garlic is unloaded off the harvest racks and spread out on the rails inside the shed. The two-by-four sleepers, which you double for the proper spacing, allow enough ventilation between layers to dry the leaves, no matter how high the stack. The temporary racks can be built up a layer at a time as high as you can reach, in my case about twenty-four layers or six feet. Our acre and a half of garlic, conveyed to the shed in fifteen harvest racks, will translate into about eighty to a hundred running feet of drying rack, five or six feet high, and about six feet wide. Similar arrangements can be devised to dry non-bolting garlic, leaves and all, if the plants are to be braided—or even to cure topped bulbs, which if heaped in a box or otherwise enclosed will begin to mold from the effects of transpiration. No matter what, garlic must always be able to breathe.

If the weather is hot and dry at harvesttime, the temporary stacking may not be necessary. Or it will be necessary only for those plants whose leaves are still green. The harvest racks can be directly unloaded to the storage rack that runs along the north end of the shed, against a cool cement block wall. It too is a lay-up and knock-down construction made up of two-by-fours and cement blocks. Chicken wire holds the bulbs a few inches away from the cement wall, allowing air circulation. The lowermost bulbs rest on a strip of plastic, to isolate them from moisture in the dirt floor. The seedpods are held up off the ground by a long row of two-by-fours laid on top of cement block pillars.

In effect, the thirty-foot long storage rack is a longer and taller version of the mobile harvest racks. Here the garlic plants will remain throughout the rest of the summer. In the fall, following planting, what's left will be sorted into what we'll keep for arrangements and what we'll sell off as eating garlic at our November open house. What's left after that goes under layers of old sleeping bags and tarps for the winter.

Unloading and stacking garlic is good work for the heat of the afternoon. Late June and early July can be hot until the afternoon thunderheads move in from the west, and though the shed seems hotter than outdoors at least it's shady. I do much of the stacking myself, so many racks an afternoon. Sometimes Rose Mary will help, or Adam and Kate when they're at home for vacation.

Stacking garlic is the kind of meditative labor with endless repetitions I find particularly pleasant: a field of garlic, once again to be lifted and moved, bit by bit, to accumulate into yet another transformation. Think of trying to do it in a hurry, all at once, by a deadline, and the work becomes hopeless. Lose yourself in the gesture, each bunch of garlic carefully lifted, pods disentangled, each board of the rack thoughtfully placed, each bunch spread out just so, and the task can reward you with its soothing rhythms first and then, later, with a sense of satisfaction, and even amazement.

I work in shorts and sandals, hatless and shirtless and gloveless except when handling the rough lumber with which I assemble each new layer of the rack. It is a time when I finally slough off the last of the aches and pains of winter and spring, sweat them out, flex them away. Now is when I inhabit my body again, fill it out, study its sensations, explore its subtly diminishing limits. I take pleasure in working in contact with the bulbs and stalks, the hot air, the dusty earth, the fragrant pine boards, and learn again how to move with economy and even a certain grace as I transfer again these tons of bulb and stalk and seedpod a handful at a time, bunch by bunch, until the task is finally done, and the harvest racks are emptied and ready to be parked for another year down in the orchard.

The harvest heals. It gives a sense of that wealth that only a stack of garlic or a pile of firewood or manure can represent, or a pickup loaded with baskets of flowers or heaped high with gourds or pumpkins or winter squash. Such is the abundance that can be surprisingly produced by a few plans, some seeds, some work, some waiting. This is wealth that has not yet been driven through the filters of abstraction and stripped of its sensual and material qualities.

The garlic pile will soon undergo a transformation into goods we take to market, scattering eventually into households everywhere. Yet besides the ways in which the market will value it by the pound or stalk or by the bunch, the pile contains worth of a more directly sustaining sort. A portion of the pile will become seed. It will return to the earth in less than three months to resume the biological cycle. Some of the garlic will enter the household as food, as a spice,

[170]

indeed as a medicine. Some of it will pass into the hands of those who work with us as shares in the abundance we preside over, and as gifts to friends.

But above all in the long garlic stack, which resembles some sort of low thatched shelter in the depths of the shed, there lies the promise of another year or another decade of such labor, or even more: an invitation to usefulness that nothing else so forthrightly poses.

This is your task, the garlic says, this is your job, and you can have it as long as you can walk, as long as you can bend, as long as you can see, as long as you can imagine.

Little else in the world I inhabit speaks as clearly as this.

*

IV

SUMMER:

EXCHANGE

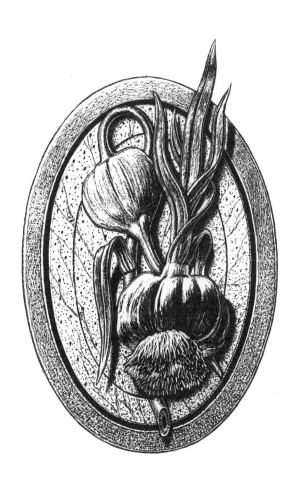

※

31

SORTING

PER POUND, garlic will often be the most expensive field crop in the produce section of your local supermarket.

A portion of the high cost of garlic lies in the fact that 8 to 10 percent of each harvest must be put back into the ground. Another portion lies in the fact that garlic must be handled a half-dozen times or more from planting to market.

Some of these steps are common to nearly all crops and others are specific to garlic alone. In large operations many will be highly mechanized, but then in order to handle the volume systems of brokers and wholesalers must be called into play.

By virtue of its size our small operation needs no intermediaries. We handle our "market grade" garlic eight times from planting to market, and we sell it by the pound for somewhat above the supermarket average but below the cost of organically grown garlic sold in a health food store. Our "*ristra* grade" garlic (from the Spanish for "string") is handled two more times. Once to make up into a bunch of a half to three-quarters of a pound, and then to be decorated with dyed jute twine, burlap, a pottery medallion, a few stalks of wheat, rye, or sorghum. Our simplest arrangement will sell at nearly ten times the per-pound value of garlic in it, and our fanciest arrangement at nearly twenty times. The last are Rose Mary's specialty, and they feature additional adornments of chile, dyed gourds, strawberry popcorn, themselves handled several times in the course of being sorted and cleaned and dried.

In the early days of all this I did most of the garlic sorting and bunching. Of the various farm jobs, it is one I think of as tedious—at least for someone who would rather be doing something more active and varied or with more dramatic results. You sit in a chair, or stand, surrounded by boxes of uncleaned garlic, from which you first cut the seed tops—they go in another box—and then sort into ristra grade and market grade. From the market grade you cut off the stalks and roots with pruning shears, then slough off the dirty outer skin, then toss the bulbs into the market box. For the ristra grade, you leave the stalk on but rub off the dried leaves, trim off roots, rub off just enough skin to produce a silvery white bulb. If too much comes off or if the remaining skin splits, then off with the stalk and into the market box. There is also a junk garlic box for bulbs that have been cut or damaged, and these will be later sorted through again for usable cloves in the kitchen or to give away to one of the kitchens of the homeless shelters in Santa Fe or Taos.

Cleaning and sorting are what you can do in the afternoon when it's too hot to be out in the sun—but it's still hot in the garlic shed, and dusty, and there's always the problem of how to set your work up in such a way that the repetitive motions don't give you a backache or blisters, or how to comfortably move boxes of garlic in and out of the shed through the narrow aisles of trestle tables laden with sorted garlic and ristras waiting to go to the shop.

In this I am most amateurish, and the garlic shed is

where we suffer from the inefficiencies of having found ourselves by imperceptible increments in the business of manufacturing a product. By imperceptible increments, also, the shed has become the province of Rose Mary and the neighbor women who work for her, Alice and Susie and Kiva, at the various stages of processing and production, while I remain the master of fields and machinery, of planting and harvesting, irrigating and cultivating. There are overlappings, however: we all plant and we all harvest together, the garlic at least, while for flowers I take the younger members of the processing crew out to do the picking but do not myself participate in the later flower-bunching in the shed.

The division of labor was never consciously decided on. Perhaps it represents the invisible tug of many traditions. To what extent it falls along a gender axis which defines who will do the more sedentary work, who the more physically active work, remains one of the mysteries. But it is very strong. After ten years or so, there is something one could call the culture of the garlic shed, consisting of a weave of gossip, of keeping up with the news of the extended families, the births, deaths, marriages, divorces, graduations, illnesses, travels, accidents, books read and movies seen, a sifting through the large and small events of our small valley that goes on for hours each day, all summer long, in English and Spanish. Some years back at the Santa Fe Farmers' Market, a woman customer announced in front of my stand that in South America where she came from garlic was used to stop gossiping. This has not been our experience.

There are conflicting claims on the garlic pile. If the harvest has been a good one, then we're always short of market grade because most of it can go into ristras for the shop. More labor intensive, the arrangements are a way to give work to our neighbors and our own kids and their friends, for whom a part-time job on the farm is an agreeable way to spend the summer. A poor-quality crop will give us more market grade than we need, and not enough for ristras. Toward August an additional claim arises, when we must begin setting aside the better garlic for planting—and when other growers approach us with requests for planting stock.

The division of labor extends to the selling. The retail shop in Taos is Rose Mary's territory and it's where she tends her display of garlic arrangements and wreaths of dried flowers she has made herself, along with my stained gourds and books, and the pottery and wines of the two Johnson families with whom we share the shop space in an informal cooperative, plus the various artifacts all our college-age children have made and whose sales go to help them through school. There Rose Mary keeps up with her friends, chats up travelers from all over the world, exchanges news with neighboring shopkeepers, harangues cops too quick to write parking tickets. She commiserates with sellers of raffle tickets who ply the shops during the desperate slow weeks of late winter and early spring, the old Pueblo Indians selling silver jewelry, the drunks and derelicts seeking handouts, tourists asking directions and tips on where to eat lunch or dinner and where to find a restroom.

Such is her market once a week, a small shop in the downstairs of a brown concrete building on the Plaza in Taos. There she launches a ton or more of our garlic out into the world each year, and there is where it leaves her hands to begin long trips by car and by air, to some final resting place on walls or window frames in distant living rooms and kitchens.

Perhaps the arrangements will be looked at for a few months, perhaps a year, and then they will become dusty and fade into the general clutter. On a few the cloves will be broken off one by one to be cooked and eaten, and eventually there will be nothing left but a bundle of stalks tied by some twine and a pottery medallion stamped with an image of a bulb of garlic, a stoneware memory of what was once alive in a patch of earth perhaps thousands of miles away. And no doubt a few of our customers will find something distinctive in the taste of our top-setting bulbs or will be pleased at the ease with which they peel, and they will put aside a few cloves to plant in their gardens in the fall.

This of course is what the garlic is banking on. And why in some deep sense it has urged us into celebrating it with these festooning and retailing exertions: to end its unnatural sojourn in the atmosphere and regain the context it has lost.

With the aid of RVs or jet airliners, the journey of ten thousand miles resumes. Anything or anyone can serve the bulb: conquistador, hippie, writer, or retiree. No distinctions are made. The only border that counts is the one we all stand on and which, with our elaborate steel tools, we assist the bulb in the labor of its final crossing.

*

3 2

BUYING AND SELLING: THE POUND WEIGHT OF THE REAL, CONTINUED

I HAVE NEVER been very good at selling.

There was the business of the Model T, bought for ten dollars, sold a year later for five. I was twelve or thirteen. The school friend in question had already got a good start in working these things out. He had sold at ten, then bought back at five a year later, with a transmission thrown in.

Much later as a beginning writer who had just banged out a lightweight satirical novel in five summer weeks on a Greek island in an old house with a view of the Turkish coast, I was bewildered by the lack of correspondence between this modest effort and the small fortune I received for the manuscript, which came to be valued at about a dollar a word. Those near me either gloried in the coup or scorned the success as too easy: this was akin to speculating in the stock market or playing the lottery.

Still later when the easy writing money ran out and when the easy writing got harder, Rose Mary and I found ourselves peddling our vegetables at the farmers' markets in Santa Fe and Taos. This was at the opposite end of the spectrum—where you can despair at the vast effort required to grow a field of vegetables for which you will receive relatively little money, and never much of it at once. Over the course of the next ten years we tried all kinds of ways to gain a return on our labor more nearly approximating the good old days of a dollar a word, selling first to restaurants, then wholesaling to roadside stands, then selling at craft fairs, and finally settling into our own retail outlet.

About 1985, for reasons somewhat obscure to me at the time, I decided to go back to the farmers' markets on my own, leaving responsibility for the shop in Rose Mary's hands. The first years back at the markets I had little to sell besides garlic and onions. Nor was it easy for me to do it alone. I had come to depend on Rose Mary's melodious, questioning voice which always causes people to pause and look up from what they're doing. I had been the grower and the driver, the organizer of boxes, the packer and unpacker of pickup and station wagon, the one who put up and took down the stand. And the one who stood back and let her do the selling.

The first summers at the Santa Fe and Los Alamos markets were trying. A customer who later became a friend described how I would sit or pace behind my little stand of onions and garlic, a tall and forbidding presence, an angry or despairing expression clouding my face. In fact I was miserable. I was a solitary island of self-absorbed gloom surrounded by people buying and selling and having a good time at it. Eventually after sufficient pain I learned to busy myself when things were slow by straightening the stand or the back of the truck and chatting with neighboring farmer-sellers. Eventually I learned not to put my ego out there on the stand with my produce, and to engage with my customers as people, not as money dispensers, and to pay attention to what they were saying—or rather, how they were uttering the stock phrases and platitudes that accompany any exchange. It took me several seasons to see the markets as places of sociability and conviviality and thus as relief from the more regimented and solitary aspects of the farm. And as I relaxed, customers began to feel at ease and would stop to chat and browse through the produce. Whether they bought or not became less important. What they were looking for or needed or liked or disliked became more interesting, and even whether they wanted to be pitched to or not, along with all those other signals they will emit, saying everything from "I know exactly what I want" or "I just want to know how much I owe you" to "I need somebody to talk to."

At one of the markets not long ago I asked a twelve-year-old friend to mind the stand while his father and I settled down on the tailgate to catch up with each other's news. There was a lull and I knew the boy was capable of dealing with the odd half a pound of garlic that might now and then be handed to him to weigh and price. But he objected. In a slightly panicked voice, he said: "I've never sold anything before."

At his age, and even much later, it would have been my protest as well. In our society the young are trained early to buy. Selling comes later. We also subscribe to the fiction that it's not something everybody has to do, preferring to think of ourselves as only buyers and consumers. Most people are perhaps unaware of the degree to which working at a job or a profession is selling yourself by the hour, the week, the month, the year—no different in essence than selling yourself by the ounce, the pound, the ton, in tens of thousands of separate transactions individually conducted, face-to-face.

A taint of disrepute haunts all exchange, perhaps because most exchange is seen as inequitable or fraudulent or magical—or manipulated from afar by powerful interests and laden with hidden costs, overhead, kickbacks. The specialist at the pinnacle of a professional career need never see the cash or checks that are banked in his name. It might be good social therapy if the analyst of the soul or the surgeon of the heart were obliged in person to receive fee and to write out receipt, so that it would remain clear throughout who was at who's service.

All this circles around the question of how to make a living—or more interestingly, an honest living, or a relatively honest living, in these times.

All human livings in industrial society are ultimately based on agricultural production and mineral extraction. One of the ways these processes are transferred upward and outward is through endless cycles of buying and selling. Which is to say that one cannot live in this kind of world without being involved in these cycles, nearly or remotely. Something of this was in my mind when I decided to go back to peddling our produce off the back of the truck at the markets. I wanted to be closer to an elemental process of human society, one which I had regarded with a degree of middle-class daintiness. Unconsciously, like many, I had aspired to the condition of always being a buyer, never a seller, always an eater, never a washer of dishes, always a wearer of clothes, never a washer of laundry, which was why I found it so painful at first to be out there on the front line, on the other side of the business.

For many, buying and selling also can seem to open a wound in the social fabric, over the chronic doubt about the reality of bits of metal and rectangles of paper and magnetic impulses that compose the grand collective fantasy known as money—the chronic doubt whether money is more real than the goods and services we provide and obtain for it.

But that perhaps is the point. Buying and selling can be seen as negotiation over what is real. Permanent negotiation, if you will, because such realities are transitory and must constantly be renegotiated, must be kept suspended, must be passed back and forth, must be planted and harvested again and again. Paradoxically, in the matter of exchange, the absolute lies in the cycle, in the flow, and in the forever-shifting rules that regulate the flow.

There is something magical in the transformations of exchange, in the metamorphoses of buying and selling. They are analogous to the transformations of the biological cycle through spore into mushroom, or seed into plant, or ovum into animal and back, alternating stages of idea and material efflorescence.

There are those who are disturbed by the lack of correspondence between money and goods, as indeed nearly everyone is at one time or another. Now and then a wound in the fabric of exchange opens, and we seem to see nothing but meaningless tokens and symbols. Yet we are far less troubled, if at all, by the lack of correspondence between objects and words or even between words and the grander abstractions which seem to rule most lives.

The distinctly human power lies in abstraction, a kind of going to seed, analogous to the way we can move a field of wheat across a continent in a burlap sack on our backs, or carry a redwood tree, a chestnut, an oak, across the ocean in our pockets. Language, images, numbers: these are the human seeds or spores by which we reconstitute ourselves anywhere in the world, back into materiality.

At times it seems very odd. I go to town with a pickup truck full of garlic and flowers and vegetables, and with an anxious heart. A few hours later I return with an empty truck and a sense of boundless promise—because I know that the exchange is still working, that my customers still want what I can grow and take to market, and that we all still believe in the engraved paper and disks of silver-clad copper, we still believe in the abstractions by which we manipulate material realities; we still believe, despite all our differences and quarrels, in ourselves and each other.

Every time you go to market you relive the story of Jack and the Beanstalk: you trade the family cow for worthless beans, but if you plant the beans, you can grow the vine by which you climb to the heavens to slay the giant or vampire that tyrannizes the community. Because you go to market, because you take the chance, because you take the elemental dare again and again, the community lives, prospers, survives.

33

THE CITY

No DOUBT every farmer has had this thought: "I planted the seeds, I cared for the plants, I harvested the crop, I did all these things, and now I just wish it would sell itself"—as if so much virtuous effort were expended in the "real work" of production that the rest should follow automatically. And indeed, in the largest agricultural sectors, those controlled by corporations and regulated by the government, the sale is virtually automatic. For the small farmer, however, finding a market can be a never-ending quest.

Across the river from my place there leans a potato digger, rusting, next to a driveway. A couple of years ago I was taken up to another village to look at a two-row transplanter parked in the weeds against a barbed-wire fence. Both pieces of equipment are remains of an agricultural co-op that was set up with government funding in the late sixties. In a village down river there stands the huge apple-packing shed of another ill-fated co-op. Filing cabinets and cardboard boxes containing agendas and minutes and financial statements for such organizations must still exist in offices and closets and attics all over the northern counties of New Mexico. Over the past twenty years I have been invited to countless meetings to propose agricultural cooperatives of one sort or another. None have got off the ground. I was even active in advancing the idea of an arts and craft and agricultural co-op that would operate as a roadside stand in the late 1970s—until the numbers became so conspicuously unreal that I was persuaded to abandon the idea. The problem was overhead. The twenty or thirty artisans and farmers who had banded together over the project simply didn't generate enough income to be able to tax themselves to rent a building and support a paid manager.

Not long afterward I awoke to the fact that a "cooperative" had been functioning quite well since the late sixties on virtually no overhead, without paid staff, on a minuscule budget, without public assistance or subsidy other than the parking lot that was turned over to its use twice a week, and that I was even a member of it: the Santa Fe Farmers' Market.

Of course it was not a true cooperative in which farmers pool their production in order to become stronger players in a regional or national market. But such a model may not be appropriate for an area of small subsistence farms in a fickle climate where the fruit crop can be decimated year after year or the chile-growing season rendered exasperatingly short. The farmers' market was more like a confederation of small growers who knew they would always be small or wished to remain so—yet nonetheless cooperative in the sense that they had organized themselves to sell together, on the principle that a parking lot of fifty small farmers is far more likely to attract a crowd than a solitary seller.

So here it was, a functioning cooperative of sorts, operating without the large public subsidies which had floated so many more grandiose and idealistic schemes—and which had sunk like stones the moment the subsidies ended. But such ideas had interested me. I had gone to all those meetings in which tenured bureaucrats celebrate the virtues of free enterprise, until I finally grasped that such meetings were the stuff of bureaucrats' careers.

So I became involved in the Santa Fe Farmers' Market. I got myself elected to the board. Then I got myself elected as president.

One of the main advantages of presiding over meetings is that you have to stay awake. You also get to choose the time and place of the next meeting, which helps increase your general alertness. Most people crave sleep above all and so are content to delegate the awakeness function to another.

What I discovered was that the farmers' market was one of those things that everyone took more or less for granted, without realizing the enormous potential to hold in place and perhaps even transform the rural landscape that fed it, and perhaps even to re-articulate relations between city and country, in a town that was growing too fast not only for its own good but for the good of the traditional Hispanic villages within its economic sphere, including the one I lived in.

I don't know whether this is exactly what my garlic had in mind, as it were. But in order to grow garlic you need land and water, and a place to sell; and the one perpetual danger is that while you feed your city with the products of your labor and your land and water, the city will grow so fat and demanding that sooner or later it will claim your land and water for its own uses, saying, "Forget the garlic, we can get it cheaper somewhere else." The farmers' market, while most obviously providing a marketplace, also is an organization by which you can convey and promote the claims and the needs of the rural small farmer within the city itself.

But as ever it is more complex than that. Twice a week July to November, by means of the farmers' market, I negotiate with the city. I show the city what my earth can produce, I feed it, I listen to its worries and fears, to the on-going debates by which it defines what it is, I note the shifting details that indicate the direction of its change. Because I have no city I am only half a man by the ancient dictum; so in going to it, with my produce, I also wish to complete myself. Growing garlic is a way for me to know the polis and become a citizen of it. And because the person who grows no garden is only half a human, a more modern prejudice, when the city comes to me, and to my stand, it is perhaps ultimately for the same reason, to fill out, complement, complete.

Santa Fe's demon is tourism. The city is flattered by tourism, enraged by it, enriched and impoverished by it, structured and confused by it, developed and ruined by it, obsessed by it. I like to think of the Santa Fe Farmers' Market as being the one regular downtown event not staged for touristic reasons, but in these days, and in Santa Fe, such a claim can easily be woven into the promotional machinery and turned inside out. And perhaps like most of my fellow citizens, I am ambivalent about the obsession. You may argue that cities have always been machines for concentrating wealth and power: this is the breathless urban enterprise to which all have contributed over the past few millennia, and which has so successfully resisted all other claims for better forms of social organization. I will say that I am the center of my little farm fifty miles north of Santa Fe, and that I even carry a certain weight within my village of a thousand souls, but I must also acknowledge, however reluctantly, that the city will always be the ultimate organizing force of my economic life.

But I come from California where cities have been eating their agricultural landscape for three generations. Three generations ago, all of my family was in agriculture. Housing tracts and freeways and shopping malls have dropped their concrete nets over land that once supplied most of the country with oranges, grapefruit, lemons, and limes. Now I am the only one of my generation in farming—and not in California.

Buying and selling are unfortunately not just about transformations back and forth through the material and the abstract. Exchange throws up side effects—or primary effects, depending on your point of view—that redistribute wealth and alter the environment. Ultimately exchange has to do with justice.

The farmer who wants his crops to sell themselves wishes to limit the horizons of the social matrix he inhabits to his fenceline or front gate, and let the rest of the world go its merry way.

A not-unnatural wish, and one which I indulge several hours each day. Farming happily allows that. Indeed, if you do not pay close and constant attention to your fields—always at the expense of what the rest of the world is up to—you risk losing all you have poured into them.

Yet the rest of the world is always there, just outside the gate. Now and then it must be heeded. It must be attended to, studied, fretted over. And taking your goods to market and selling them is a way to discover just what is out there—even at times what you can do about it—to hold your streams and woods, your ditches and fields, your patch of garlic safe against the city's long-range plans, its schemes for becoming bigger and more powerful and farther-reaching.

I remind myself that historically the city always wins. The countryside always loses. That is, until something collapses—the environment, the political structure—and everything becomes countryside again.

＊

34

STAYING HOME

I REMEMBER my father leveling the ground for the goat house. It was next to the neighbor's irrigation pond where ducks swam under a weeping willow and bullfrogs meditated in the cattails.

The site for the goat house was as far from the house as you could get, a hundred yards. I later understood this to be the first sign of trouble.

I remember being taken on a drive to inspect the prospective goat, a white broad-beamed Toggenberg. I would have been five or six. There was something about an allergy to cow's milk.

Then the preparations stopped. The goat house was never built, weeds grew on the site, no goat was ever bought. In an accepting way, I never asked why not—or no longer remember having done so. But now I can reconstruct it all. This would have been just after the end of the War. Gas rationing was over at last. The national parks in the Sierras beckoned. I can hear one of my parents' schoolteacher friends, who also lived for the long summer vacations, saying something like this: "If you get a goat, you can kiss your camping trips good-bye."

Twenty-five years later and a thousand miles away I completed that goat house myself. When Rose Mary and I moved into a rented adobe in northern New Mexico, the first thing I built was a wooden goat house out of panels of rough-sawn pine that could be easily knocked apart and reassembled elsewhere. Then we bought two does: Bobbie, an old gray Alpine-Toggenberg cross, and a frisky dark Nubian, Nancy, one of whose first doe kids we kept and called Cleo.

The goats became a center to our lives. They had to be fed and watered and milked every morning and then again every afternoon. Goats are hard on pens and their fixtures. They constantly lean, butt, climb, chew. Millennia of domestication have taught them that if they lean and rub and butt long enough, the fence will fall down, the goat house will collapse, the gate will swing open—though by then they are apt to be quite bewildered by their sudden freedom.

Goats keep you at home. Add chickens and ducks and geese, dogs and cats, a hive of bees, a vegetable garden, then a field or two, which we soon had in cultivation, and the dream of peacocks in the trees and carp in a pond, and you have even more reasons to stay at home, though nothing is quite as compelling as goats. Gardens and fields go dormant in the winter, and cats and dogs and chickens and ducks and geese can fend for themselves a day or two with minimal support from a neighbor out on a walk once a day. But with goats you almost need a live-in sitter if you wish to get away, and one familiar and sympathetic with the complex needs of the creatures, which is to say a neighbor who probably has goats of his own and therefore already enough on his hands.

But staying at home is the most ecological thing to do. There is no other way to grow your garden, tend your animals, your orchard, your streams and rivers, ponds and lakes, fences and roads, to study the accretions of time. This is of course mainly what most of humankind has done for most of history. The numbers are rapidly coming in to say that running around, driving and flying, on the scale now considered socially acceptable and even fashionable, is something the planet cannot much longer support.

Staying home is hauling water and chopping wood, mending your fences, hoeing your row, planting your tree, digging out your ditches, raising your children, milking your goats. For those who stay at home, there is no figure of speech here, no metaphor: these are lists of the real chores by which the notion of home, both of house and of landscape, is made and defined.

I quickly gave up bees. My patience was of another sort than that needed for beekeeping. We raised goats through our children's childhood, then gave them up too. I tore down the goat house, pulled up the fenceposts. But by then the garden had become a small farm, and the list of chores was endless, and there were reasons enough to stay home.

We kept the cats and the dogs and the geese, animals more tolerant of the human fashion of the day. In a sense they are stand-ins for an older way. And whenever we leave, insisting on our mobility, they tell us we are leaving—the dogs can readily distinguish the sullen haste with which we make for the car or the pickup from the loose-jointed shamble out the front door that says we're going for a walk down to the river, and from their pen the geese will salute their joy at the prospect of being let out on the grass for a while, or their disappointment when we head the other way.

And then, several hours or a day later when we return from the city, they tell us with their barks and cries that where we have come back to is home; and they may wonder, in their way, not understanding the urgent pull of human fashion, why we ever left.

*

35

THIRD WORLD
SUMMERS

I'M SIX-FEET-THREE.

I regularly consider the ironies. Camus said that the man who fears becoming a thief is the one who ends up a bank teller.

Six-foot-three is not the best height for pulling garlic or picking flowers or cutting lettuce or spinach, to be dealing with the pound weight of the real at ground level.

Yet every summer I spend the better part of two days a week doing what the better part of the laboring world does, which is bending over, stooping down, crouching, at times even sitting, to pick, to snap, to cut stem or stalk close to the ground. What must be picked, cut, pulled on a typical August Wednesday or Friday for the Thursday and Saturday markets is roughly as follows:

First there are approximately twenty-five hundred statice blossoms each of the two days, half of the field, about half an acre, approximately one blossom or spray or panicle per plant. I don't pick them all. I pick about six hundred. Daughter Kate home from college picks about six hundred. Galilee Carlisle, also home from college, the same college, picks about six hundred. She and her family may wonder if they are in some deep bondage to my family, because it was her parents, and her aunt and uncle, who helped us make our adobe bricks twenty years ago. Kiva Duckworth picks six hundred. Her parents were agents, among others, of our moving to New Mexico those twenty years ago. And sometimes son Adam, also six feet plus, and sometimes a visiting friend of his or Kate's—who may wonder what summer madness he or she has stumbled into—turns up to give us a hand.

We'll spend perhaps three hours at this labor, eight to eleven, carrying our wooden bushel baskets up and down the rangy, bright rows. Statice is a relatively new crop for us. After several trials we started growing it in quantity about five years ago, and we've all learned together how each color has its own habit and character. In its maturity the plants resemble giant dandelions with multiple flower buds unfurling from a central crown, and a fully mature panicle will reach a height of two feet. Yellow is the color that blossoms earliest in the season, and its tough stalks must be cut with clippers, a tedious job we all do together before moving into the rows of other colors; it's also the first color to peter out in autumn, running rapidly from chronic surplus to chronic shortage. The rows of peach and apricot also require clippers, and their sprays are easy to miss in the low early morning light, yet they withstand rains and frost better than the other colors. Pink and purple don't open as fully and are best picked somewhat immature; and like light blue and white, the sprays can be snapped off near the base of the stalk between thumbnail and index finger, giving you a genuine green thumb. White shows the most variation in its blooming: some plants will produce wide expansive blooms while others will be tight and reluctant in their opening.

Everyone has their favorite color for picking, which

they will cover the most thoroughly. Light blue sings to me in a piercing, haunting way but I often end up picking peach and apricot because I feel no one goes over these "old lady colors"—as later mutterings in the shed will have them—as well as I do. The only defect of the flowers lies in their lack of scent—and in that odd fish-like odor of the green juice that comes to cover your fingers after a morning of picking.

As late as eight or nine on a summer day the white-blossoming swaths of buckwheat, rising from the former garlic fields, and the acre of statice, will still be cool and damp, particularly after an evening rain shower. The morning dew and the damp and often muddy earth invite us to leave shoes and sandals at the edge of the field and work in bare feet. Torpid bumblebees will just be waking up in the blooms. Carefully we shake them off into neighboring clumps of picked buds: we know from experience that they can still sting even if half-asleep. An unusual spider spotted in the depths of a plant will cause all of us to drop baskets and climb over rows of blossoms to take a look. Then we resume our weaving, our threading work up and down the long bright rows. The young women call out their news and stories as they draw apart; and then their voices lower and there is laughter as they move together in the rows, or when they gather momentarily at the pickup and the tractor to exchange a full basket of flowers for an empty.

It will be a twenty-five-bushel morning or a thirty-bushel morning depending on the weather. Picked by color the baskets will fill the back of the pickup and the tractor front loader and rear lift box, and we'll parade them flamboyantly down the dirt road and up the driveway to the shed. In another era we would sing a celebratory peasant song, but I can think to hear it only faintly now in deepest memory, and it lies beneath the groans and sighs that are the expressions of flushed faces and aching backs and sore fingers and deep ripping thirsts: oh how pretty these flowers, but oh how much work they are, and the work we've done is only a third of what yet must be done with them. Each of those twenty-five hundred blossoms has yet to be trimmed, arranged, bunched, banded, sleeved; work which Rose Mary, Kate, Susie, Alice, Kiva, and Galilee, plus house guests and friends who have dropped by for the day, will carry on to late afternoon, often into the evening, often resuming the next morning. In this manner the thirty-bushel baskets of solid colors will kaleidoscope into 150 variegated bouquets, and into tall heaps of dark green stalks, bent blooms, unopened buds that will be fished through to make up a dozen or so mini-bouquets before being carried off to the compost pile.

I leave this work to the women, and am much-mocked for doing so, while I return to the fields to continue my morning's work of stooping and bending. Next there are the Walla Walla onions; I will walk up and down the rows and pull them and carry them up to the front loader, and filling it to overflowing; some three hundred fat onions in all, a pound or better each, my pungent trophies, which I can carry ten at a time by their still-green necks up to the tractor. This long-day onion does quite well in our intermediate-day zone. In order to have a continuous supply for the market from July into September I don't thin the fall-seeded crop, which serves to hold the bulbs back from maturing all at once. I can fill the loader in about half an hour of pulling the fattest bulbs from half the patch Wednesday, the other half on Friday. The loader bucket, four feet wide and a foot and a half deep, serves as a conveniently adjustable and cleanable washing tub back up at the driveway turnaround, where I hose dirt and loose skin off the bulbs and pack them untopped into wooden bushel boxes, plump yellow fishes with blue-green tails. The eight to ten boxes go into the pickup camper as the first and lowest layer to be loaded for market; and for the rest of the afternoon the aroma of sweet onions swirls around the driveway with each passing gust of wind.

By noon or one o'clock six-foot-three has stooped and bent and crouched to three-foot-three or less a thousand times. I have often thought what a beautiful, productive world this would be if all our joggers and weight-lifters would put their energies into gardening instead. But never mind. The back aches. The joints are rubbery. But when we're lucky, which is to say organized, we can take a two-hour lunch and siesta. Rose Mary and Kate and the women can then resume the interminable flower bunching in the shed, exchanging sarcastic mutterings, and I can go back to the fields to pull a hundred beets, Green Top Bunching, a variety I favor for its abundant tops, a hundred knee bends, back bends; cut a couple of dozen heads of lettuce, Buttercrunch, a resilient Bibb type I've grown for decades—a couple of dozen more foldings and unfoldings, by now in what I hope will be the shade of late afternoon thunderheads rising to the west. The tractor loader bucket serves again for wheelbarrow *cum* washing tub. If the afternoon is still hot and bright, I'll stack the boxes of beets and lettuce in the shade of the worktable under the weeping willow at the driveway turnaround, or if cloudy and cooling I'll load them directly into the camper, give them a last hosing down, then cover them with the blue planks that do double duty first as flooring for the second layer of boxes and baskets in the camper and later as the countertop of our stand at the market. A bucket of lettuce leaves goes to the geese, who celebrate loudly as they wolf down the succulent, sweet leaves.

Add then a few boxes of early winter squash, a dark green acorn squash or Jersey Golden Acorn—my best-selling squash until 1991, when the seed was withdrawn from the market because of a high proportion of bitter fruit—which will complete the bottom layer of boxes in the pickup, and which I load from a stack of boxes in the shade, perhaps a hundred one- to two-pound squash in all, picked earlier in the week. They come now as a gift, needing only to be shunted from one place to another, not adding to the grand total of stoopings. And even later in the season, pumpkins, one or two per box, also picked on an earlier day of the week.

The momentum of the day sweeps us restlessly through dinner and then coffee taken Roman-style reclining on the couch, our minds, Rose Mary's and mine, ticking off the things yet to do before dark if possible and after dark if not; and so, even as we rest, the mind bends, stoops, cuts, carries, washes, clips, bands, packs.

The air is cooling. The evening air is rich with motes wafting groundward at oblique angles, making it palpable and almost thick, this air, like the water of a perfectly clean aquarium. Barn swallows with their elegantly forked tails skim the earth at eye level, a pair at a time. At the treetops, at the tops of the light green cottonwoods, cliff swallows work the middle air, and occasionally a fluttering bat; and higher, so high you wonder what can be up there, nighthawks, seeming to be all wing, crying their high-pitched alarms, make their sweeping, darting course; above them will be only the vultures slowly circling as they ready to drop themselves to their roost; and above them perhaps a gold-tinged jet-trail chasing the sun; and yet higher a moon, an evening star to the west.

This is the spanning sky above as I go back out into the field for a last time, in the cooler air and lengthening shadows, to work the rows of sweet Genovese basil, to cut back a fourth or a fifth of the thousand plants, whose smell, and perhaps the limpid sky, its air—these alone can fuel the tired body, in this last hour of crouching and clipping and carrying. Sometimes I will have help. Rose Mary will carry the boxes while I clip, or Kate, or my father in the weeks he is here, moving them down the rows to the pickup or the tractor, and then if I'm running late back at the washing stand, where I sort and band the seven or eight hundred stalks into a hundred quarter-pound bunches, racing against the dark, someone will dip the bunches into buckets of water, giving them a cleansing, refreshing swirl, and pack them into wooden bushel boxes; and as the aroma of basil plumes out over the driveway, the last of daylight slips away, and darkness descends.

I switch on the shed floodlights. Rose Mary will be arranging the last of the baskets of statice, seven or eight white-sleeved bouquets per basket, and will carry me the ones she wants to go to market, which I will slide into the camper on top of the blue planks, pushing and nudging them into the depths with a cut-down hoe I use for such purposes to save my knees and spare me yet more bending. We can fit eleven bushel baskets into the camper and three more behind the seat of the extended cab, and one more if Rose Mary is in a mood to carry it on her lap during the hour drive to Santa Fe the next morning. Two or three lug boxes of market garlic go on the floor at her feet and on the seat between us. A sack of her arrangements, plus the cash box, scales, boxes of paper bags, signs, empty boxes which, upended, serve as the pillars of our stand, a water jug, and two tool boxes will be tucked behind the front seat and in the camper.

The lifting day is over. I have folded and unfolded myself perhaps two thousand times. I could envy short, wiry people if it weren't for what I could imagine as a passion for tall ladders and unreachable fruit. I know too well I could make choices that would spare me these days where I must make obeisance to the earth thousands of times. Yet, in this, I know inescapably my roots. Save the metaphor for fancier use. I do by choice what much of the rest of the world must do by dire, brutal necessity. This does not wash me clean of my share of privilege as a citizen of the wealthiest and most consumingly rapacious country in the world, but through this labor I know in bone and joint and sinew what it is to live that life with windows on no other; lives upon which all of us ultimately live, because those backs and knees and joints are always down there, at the menial tasks that add up, when multiplied by the billions, the trillions, to the leisure, and repose, and peacefulness, the order, where we others live.

Several years ago, through an international exchange program, fourteen Peruvian farmers were brought to us for a day to help harvest our garlic, as part of a "hands-on" workshop. They were an effusive, friendly crew. Luck would have it that it was our drought year, the year of our worst harvest, and that by the time they arrived we were to pull the worst of our three fields. If they were not impressed with the size of our garlic, they tactfully did not show it. But I noticed how little they were interested in my collection of farm machinery in the orchard, where we gathered for a snapshot session after lunch in the house. They used horses on their farms. A tractor was something they could never think of buying in their lifetimes, let alone any of the implements. But this was something that caused them apparently no grief, no envy. They were the happy ones. I was the one who did not know how to say what was weighing me down, that I was sorry I owned so much; and even, that I would own more; and even, possibly, because I would own more, they might own even less.

Picking day is over. I will have hosed down the Dodge and cleaned the windows and checked the oil in the afternoon. Now, before I shut off the shed lights, I make sure the vents and windows are closed and the heater set to the "on" position, simple finishing touches which if left until the haste of early morning can become exasperating problems to one in a fragile state, as Rose Mary and I will both be. A last look at the special order list—did I remember the purple bouquets for the wedding, the extra bunches of basil for a customer who plans to freeze a winter's supply of pesto sauce this weekend, the yellow statice with long stems for Mrs. Bradbury?—and then I can go inside.

My mind is papered with lists. Lay out clothes for the morning. Set up the thermos and coffeemaker, fill the kettle, set the table for breakfast. Lay out reading matter, which will help me eat at an hour that I have little interest in food. Check that the alarm is set for 4:30—a late hour, given that there are farmers going to Santa Fe who must leave at 2:00 and 3:00 A.M. It seems odd to be inside the cool earthen walls, crepitations pulsing through the windows, to be contained within the sudden simplification that consists of being inside a house—with the knowledge of all that is still out there, outside, in the fields. The slightest excuse will send me back outside again, into the dark with a flashlight, to check that I turned off the water somewhere, packed the scales, the paper bags.

We sink into bed at nine-thirty or ten. Whether we will be rigid with fatigue or strangely relieved and relaxed will have something to do with how we have inscribed those thousands of gestures into our bodies over the course of this day, and how we will orchestrate the inevitable fears that gather the moment the lights go out: that we won't be able to sell all we've crammed into the pickup, that people won't show up at the market, that the truck won't start or will break down on the fifty-mile drive, each of which must be patiently answered like an insistent child. Or that the phone will ring late in the night or that the dogs will bark at the skunks or coyotes all night—or will bark because they are as overstimulated from the long day as we are.

The list of worries is checked over, items dismissed or filed away somewhere for future reference. Muscles release their grip. Joints stir aimlessly. Behind my eyes I see the statice blooms again, the onions in their rows, the miniature trees of basil with shiny folded leaves. I'm picking again, cutting, bending, stooping, carrying.

Only I can watch it now like a movie as I stretch out in my bed, and let it play all night through—as I lie close to the ground, no longer six-foot-three.

＊

36

TO MARKET: SANTA FE

I HAVE WOKEN UP.

The time is perhaps 7:30 A.M. Legally I have been awake for three hours. Technically I awoke at 4:30.

In those three hours I have dressed, eaten breakfast, driven the fifty miles to Santa Fe. Rose Mary and I may even have engaged in desultory conversation of a ritual sort from our separate jiggling islands in the front seat of the Dodge pickup, basket of flowers on her lap, cup of coffee now and then touching my lips as I drive. But I have not been awake. A veil remains between the minimal mind needed to eat, drive, sip a cup of coffee, and the rest of my brain which sleeps like a baby in a crib under mosquito netting. I have piloted the heavily laden pickup down the Rio Grande canyon under the dark boulders. I have held the red needle at sixty-three through the long shadows out in the flats. I have felt the rising sun touch me on the shoulder through the glass. I will have swung into the Sanbusco Market Center parking lot on the edge of the old rail yards in the Guadalupe district of downtown Santa Fe. I will have unpacked the truck and set up the stand and greeted neighboring farmers and served a couple of dozen customers, even helped settle a dispute, all in this condition of technical wakefulness. Abruptly something clicks. The veil lifts. Ears open, and eyes, nose, taste buds. I feel the low sunlight warming my shirt. I wiggle my toes in my boots. I can focus my eyes on things—coins, bills, paper sacks, the hedge of produce and flowers that separates Rose Mary and me from our customers. We stand as amid the fragrant float of a parade, a crowd swirling past. Immediately I see there are things wrong. One of the dozen baskets crammed with statice bunches ringing the stand is empty, has tipped over. The teetering pile of Walla Walla sweet onions, bulbs stacked facing the river of foot traffic flowing past our stand, is about to topple over into a basket of flowers. The basil box between the onions and the scale is nearly empty. As is the lettuce box to the left of the scale. The garlic flat to the left of that has already been pawed over, leaving only the smaller bulbs on top and a chaff of white skin and brown roots. And where have all the paper bags gone?

Rose Mary sees it all at the same time and in a lull between customers we both scurry about to rearrange and restock the stand. A clutter of empty boxes blocks my way into the back of the pickup; I must move them out to the pavement between our truck and the Romeros' before I can pull forward the rest of the boxes full of onions, lettuce, basil, beets. The beets haven't been selling, though. People have been picking them up and saying, "Nice," but then they put them down and walk off. Did I say good morning to the Romeros? Cecilia and Paul are both leaning over their stand smiling at a customer, thanking her, slipping some chile into her basket. They're a handsome middle-aged couple who live down the road from us in the village of Velarde.

Across the way Amadeo and Rose Trujillo from Nambe Pueblo are setting up and selling at the same time, Amadeo in his gray Stetson and cowboy boots, Rose in jeans and a long-sleeved shirt. He catches my eye, gives me a short little wave, half smile, eyes rolling at some problem I can readily imagine.

The sun has risen enough to be no longer blinding. Chins up, shopping bags and baskets held a little forward, shoppers stride up and down the parking lot in search of peaches or sweet corn before they sell out, perhaps hoping to bump into old friends not just yet.

Across the way old Truman Brigham's stand is ringed by customers all patiently waiting, holding heads of lettuce and bunches of carrots and turnips and dollar bills aloft, leaning toward the figure dressed in an old gray suit coat and gray felt hat as he swivels back and forth between scale and outstretched hand. He's in his eighties, has been selling at the market since the beginning twenty years ago, or since he retired as a highway department gardener and took up farming in Española. He's always the first here, the first to set up: he must arrive at six. Occasionally I pass a head of lettuce or cabbage on the highway which I guess will have blown off the back of his open long-bed Chevy stacked high with lug boxes of produce. I admire the old people selling at the market, and I will be pleased eventually to become one of them: needed, wanted, being stood-in-line-for all morning long.

Harvey Frauenglass's low, sonorous voice sounds through a lull in the noise of footsteps, questions, distant shouts. On our other side Harvey sells fruit and cider, grown and pressed in a beautiful hillside orchard downriver from our place. The confiding, eloquent pitch with which he sells his cider is as good as the carefully blended cider itself, easily best in the market. Harvey and I are self-proclaimed members of the University of Chicago Alternative Alumni Association—a group so far of two of those graduates who have rebelled against their fancy university education, refused to become

Nobel laureates in physics and chemistry, and instead (like Socrates) gravitated to the public market.

I fluff up the bunches of basil in the tray and the rush resumes. Three customers want some of everything at once. Sue Ann Snyder arrives, throws her purse in an empty box in the back of the pickup and immediately takes over. She works as a caterer, serves as volunteer secretary to the market board, comes to help us out on Saturday mornings, and her arrival means I can steal a moment to eat a cinnamon roll bought from the stand in the middle of the parking lot. She and Rose Mary exchange quips and immediately begin giggling. Then after restocking the stand I can go for a second stroll up and down the twin rows of pickups and station wagons, tailgates down and liftbacks up, and the lines of stands made up of planks and crates and sawhorses, all laden with fruits and vegetables and plants and flowers, pies and cakes, their growers and pickers and bakers peering over the products of their labors, the harvest of their long picking days the day before. For my first stroll, made just after setting up and before the first rush of customers, I would have still been asleep, would have only nodded to farmers I now can exchange a few words with.

The sky will be a limitless cerulean blue. A faint breeze will waft through the market, and the crisp air will bear along the aroma of our basil to the next stand down where it is sold, Marcia Brenden's, and the smell of sweet onion leaves crushed under foot, even of garlic where the odd clove has fallen to the pavement and been trodden on. The crowd swirls along. Most of the faces are familiar by now but this early the names float separately, disconnected, refusing to claim their owners in an orderly manner. Here and there friends gather with laden shopping bags and baskets and form a little dam in the middle of the aisle between the rows of stands. People squeeze past, necks craning at displays the blockage has forced them near.

There is Jan Barbo, presiding over her fresh-cut delphiniums, larkspur, gladiola, and other flowers I pause to ask her the names of, her pots and tubs spilling over into Marcia's overflowing buckets of zinnia blooms. Farther down, past the cinnamon roll stand run by a local restaurant, Steve and Valerie Kaeppler are unloading the contents of their green van, baskets and boxes of statice flowers, herbs, and lettuce much like our own—though bunched and displayed more compactly and tidily than ours—and with always too many customers around them to get much of a word in. We'll talk later, if any of us have the breath left to do so.

A little further down, Abel and Susie Martinez are there with apples and chile and squash, and we quickly exchange news. Abel, a handsome fellow in regulation cowboy hat and boots, makes jokes and puns much too early in the morning, which I complain about to his warm and expansive wife, wondering how she can stand it; and we all laugh. Across the way, a relation, Aurelia Vigil, retired schoolteacher, calls out under ruffled bonnet: even though we have known each other for years, she still calls me by my last name. Next to her, shy Mrs. Cordoba waves with her sweet smile and wide dark eyes. She's of the old formal school, modest, self-effacing, generous.

Perhaps here I'll bump into Arnie Souder, our market manager, rushing back from some problem with a space assignment to his post at the entrance to the parking lot where he guides customers' cars and farmers' trucks into the parking area. He's a short, balding man recently retired from managing a 150-million-dollar division of a mining company; his slightly pouting, critical expression looks severe to those who don't know how readily he can be humored into a

broad smile and behind-the-teeth chuckle, which serve him
well as shepherd and cowpoke to the seventy-some farmers
who arrive, often anxious and ill-humored, at the small
parking lot each Tuesday and Saturday, and to the thousands
of customers hot on their heels the rest of the morning.
Walking back toward my stand we'll confer or commiserate
or exchange gossip before spinning off our separate ways, he
to a traffic jam at the entrance of the Sanbusco parking lot,
me back behind the stand where the display is half empty
again and Rose Mary and Sue both call out: "Where are the
rest of the bags?"

"Is this this year's garlic crop?" a customer wants to
know.

"Yes, ma'am, it is. Pulled end of June."

In the cramped space behind the stand the three of us
try not to step on each others' toes or knock over our cups of
coffee and keep out of the way of the scale and cash box, all
while making change and answering two questions at once.

"Are these dry?" a woman asks, holding up a bouquet
of statice.

"They are drying. They were picked yesterday," one
of us will explain. Or all three of us together. "You don't
need to put them in water."

"You don't?"

A man huddles over the garlic flats, pawing through
one and then another. "How do you make garlic keep?
What's the difference between these different kinds of garlic?
Or are they all the same?"

I explain. The top-setting, which peels easiest. The
regular California Early, which may keep a little better.
Elephant garlic, very mild, not a true garlic. I wonder
whether he'll look up and say: "But all good to keep away
vampires, right?"

[209]

In the crowd there will be the earnest, serious face of a younger well-tanned woman in shorts. She'll catch my eye.

"Is your produce organic?"

"We use no herbicides or pesticides. We fertilize with chicken manure and green manure crops."

"Then it's organic, isn't it?"

Rose Mary will answer for me. "Yes, it's very organic."

"Excuse me," someone will call out, "when should I pull up my garlic?"

"Last month," I call back.

"Oh really. But how do I know when it's ready?"

A couple of women customers shopping in convoy wedge their way up to the boxes of basil and start waving the bunches around, setting off a rush.

"I'm addicted to pesto sauce."

"Smell that basil."

"Do you have more?"

"A dollar a bunch? You're kidding. I'll take five."

Amid the crush of aggressive shoppers, an old Hispanic woman will be holding out a tiny garlic bulb in my direction, surely the smallest in the box. "How much?"

"A nickel."

Followed then by a careful search through a plastic coin purse for the exact nickel.

"*Gracias, señora. Qué vuelva.*"

So it goes until we're sold out of fresh produce at eight-thirty or nine and then sold out of flowers at ten-thirty or eleven. By then hundreds of customers and friends and farmers will have stopped by the stand, to buy, to chat, to ask a question, make a request. The pipe-smoking market treasurer, David Hall, retired Los Alamos physicist, will have paused to drop a sardonic remark about the tone of the market this particular day, report briefly on the finances. Jean Rydman, who collects our rental fees with a gentle touch, will pass by with a little wave. Pam Roy, market executive director, will shout out greetings and news as she scurries by in running gear. Jane Bendt will sidle up to the stand at some point with a worry or a problem about the market, amid a parenthesis of bad jokes. Gloria Trujillo may amble across from her stand across the way to give me news about how the publicity budget is holding up. Later in the morning David Oberstein will abruptly appear in front of the stand with a mock salute, perhaps then to report on some aberration down the line—a woman selling used clothing. "Do you think she grew it herself?" David is general manager of the company that owns the building and parking lot the market sets up on every Tuesday and Saturday from early June until early November. The owner of the property, Joe Schepps, invited us here some years back, perhaps bringing more on his head in the form of monstrous crowds than he bargained for. And later in the morning, newspaper tucked under his arm, Clark de Schweinitz will drop by for a chat about the latest move in the endless game of water rights litigation which for decades has preoccupied rural communities in the north. Up until a few years ago I served on the board of the legal services program he is the executive director of, experience which gave me a sense of how the ideal board and staff should function and how they should interrelate, and which I have tried to transfer to the smaller, more local organizations I have had a hand in. And by then I will have heard tales from farmers passing by the stand of downpours and hailstorms, flooding acequias, errant horses and cows, sleepless nights, coyotes in henhouses, plagues of grasshoppers, trucks refusing to start or stop, field hands who didn't show up, illnesses, injuries, deaths, marriages, births, accounts of a stunning moon or of a sunrise never seen before, someone in a bad mood, a lost purse, found keys, a fender-bender, no sales, a record-breaking day: the news from here, Santa Fe, and the northern counties of Rio Arriba, Taos, Los Alamos, Sandoval, San Miguel. And by then I will have downed a small thermos of coffee and a couple of sweet rolls, some juice and water, an apple or two, all on top of my five o'clock breakfast, and yet I'll still be hungry and thirsty.

And then the veil descends. I remain technically awake. But the buzzing, rubbery cast to all sensation, the tongue too large for the mouth, the heavy hands and feet, all tell me that a significant portion of my being has shut down, has passed out. Rose Mary is in a similar state. We're too tired to pack up the truck and drive away. Another greeting or request or question will come as a whiplash across my flushed face as I lean inside the camper and try to make some order of the jumble of empty boxes and baskets, no longer able to do two or three things at once. Still, there is the faint fluttering of excitement deep within: we have sold out, we have done well.

We sweep up the debris of onion tops and white garlic skins and blackening basil leaves, lock the camper, climb in the cab and count bills and checks. Then I start the engine and back slowly out through the milling crowd and drive away, heading back north through bustling streets that were so quiet and empty and cool only four hours ago. The sun is too high. The rich colors of the recent dawn are bleached, faded, powdery. The long shadows are gone.

The highway will be crowded now with people rushing out of town to the mountains and streams and lakes of the north. I will attempt to resist the spurious logic that says that if I drive fast I will remain more alert. Rose Mary and I will run back over the market morning aloud, wondering at how we sold more flowers than we expected but much less garlic. Where can we keep the bags so they'll be in easy reach of all three of us? How can we display her arrangements better? Wasn't So-and-So suddenly looking so old? But what about us? Is all this worth it? Don't ask, I tell myself. Don't look at the world through the lens of exhaustion. But when you're exhausted the hardest thing to do is turn the eye away. Foot on the accelerator, I speed us north. We have left behind the market. Its bustle can seem mindless. The fifty-mile drive back home through the hard bright sun is always too long. There's the second anticlimax of unpacking empty boxes and baskets and the few remaining bunches of pawed-over flowers, the half-empty flats of garlic.

We will eat a quick lunch and then settle in for a long nap through the heat of the afternoon in the hope that the phone won't ring and that nobody will come up the drive wanting garlic, one of those cars we passed, one of those cars now leaving town.

A cool breeze always flows through the adobe living room, even on the hottest days. I drink coffee again when I wake up, sitting by the window in the breeze. I log the accounts then, looking up last year's take for the same day. Later, Rose Mary and I will walk down the driveway and down the dirt road, through a copse of cottonwoods to a tiny sandy beach at the river. The instant face and head go under, splashing cold waters will begin to wash away the babble of those hundreds of voices and loosen the clamped muscles of fatigue, and transform the tensions of driving and talking and the strain of constantly focused linear consciousness into a diffuse glow of physical weariness that tells me I will sleep tonight and know a sense of rest again.

The veil lifts. The tiers of consciousness all flicker back into wakefulness one at a time, or in bursts, not yet all together. My spirits will rise as the shadows lengthen and the day begins to cool. Back from the river, showered and dressed, I'll ramble through the gardens and walk up the road to the other field, which will need to be tilled or mowed or cultivated or planted or irrigated tomorrow or Monday or Tuesday, and there will seem to be easily enough time for all these things before the four-day market cycle resumes again on Wednesday—though I secretly know, even as I try to hide the knowledge from myself, that those three days will be far from enough time.

Night descends. The crickets sing. I learn to hope again, and to know the restoration of the strange faith in the fragile endeavor of raising things from the earth, to accept the fragility, to accept the abundance.

I can feel the days ahead stirring in my body. They are connected, these fields, these high sunny days and warm nights, and this creature that plies them endlessly through the days.

I am awake again. It all makes sense again. I know I can go on.

37

THE ATOMIC BOMB
RING

THE THURSDAY MARKET is another matter. It takes place in another town. And I go there for other reasons.

Where I live, you go "to" Santa Fe, Española, Taos, or even Albuquerque. But when you go to Los Alamos, you always go "up to" it. And when you refer to it from my village or Santa Fe or Española you always refer to it as "up there," "up in Los Alamos," "up on the Hill."

The preposition marks the fact that Los Alamos perches above its surrounding communities on the slopes of an ancient volcano, at an altitude of seven thousand five hundred feet. The preposition also marks the town's cultural remoteness from the rest of northern New Mexico as an overwhelmingly Anglo settlement, less than fifty years old, ringed by Pueblo Indian and Hispanic villages that have been there for centuries. It may also touch upon the apartheid-like structure of the town, which is made up of a resident white scientific and managerial elite served by a largely Hispanic blue-collar work force that commutes up a twisting mountain road from the Española Valley and its many surrounding villages, including my own forty-five miles to the northeast.

Roughly the same rules apply for selling at the Los

Alamos Farmers' Market as at any other farmers' market, more or less. And the reasons for growing for such a market, and for selling at one, remain the same as elsewhere, namely that buyer and seller stand on an equal footing as producer and customer, that the selling farmers and gardeners are not agents or representatives or employees of institutions or corporations, that they are likely to be in possession of more information about their produce—and be generally willing to impart it—than the entire staff of a supermarket; and that the give-and-take of buying and selling takes place without the intervention of corporate advertising machinery, in an open space, under the sky, in an atmosphere of enhanced sensual alertness. A good market is an information system where fruits and vegetables are exchanged along with lore about how they are planted, grown, stored, cooked, and in this the Los Alamos Farmers' Market is no exception. It may also be the most beautiful farmers' market in the whole country.

The market takes place on a graveled clearing amid a grove of ponderosa pines, and everywhere you look there are pleasant views. To the west the eye sweeps through the pines and across a grassy clearing to the fitful traffic of Central Avenue as it crests a gentle rise, the highest point of the downtown area. Just beyond, in a bowl-like depression of well-trimmed lawn and weeping willows, there lies a circular pond where swim municipal geese and ducks. To the north, through the pines, there rise the steep wooded slopes of the Jemez. The mountain air of the seven-thousand-foot town is clear and crisp and often scented with the early morning smoke of piñon and juniper and pine burning in the local fireplaces.

And to the south 150 yards, across the grass, through the elms and cottonwoods and spruce, there sits the dark shape of Fuller Lodge, a splendid old building of huge logs laid flat and stood upright and bridging across each other for two stories up. It was designed by the architect John Gaw Meem in the 1920s as the centerpiece of the posh Los Alamos Ranch School which catered to the sons of wealthy easterners. The market side is the Lodge's backyard; if you go around the other side you will find a stately front porch which gives on to a band of lush grass and trees, beyond which is the downtown business district of the town of ten thousand—which for the past forty years has obstructed the view of the downward sloping Pajarito Plateau as it drops off into the Española Valley and gives way to a sweeping, a breath-filling expanse of the whole of the Sangre de Cristo Range from the Colorado border to where it ends at Santa Fe and beyond, to the Sandia Mountains above Albuquerque. There are arguably better panoramas in northern New Mexico—the view of the Jemez from San Cristobal or from Truchas, or coming down the Peñasco highway, or entering the basin above Abiquiu where Georgia O'Keeffe painted— than the one so commonly available in Los Alamos (except now from the front porch of the Lodge), but in any list it would be near the top. The school and its Lodge were taken over by the United States Army Corps of Engineers late in 1942; on one of the log columns of the porch of this rustic version of a Greek temple you will see the letters "T-81" stenciled in white, its official name and address from then on, through the rest of World War II.

The Lodge was the first headquarters of what is now Los Alamos National Laboratory, and many of the first wooden lab buildings were built around the old sinkhole that has been known as Ashley Pond ever since the mischievous Ranch School boys named it after the first director, Ashley Pond. All is lawn now, and trees, and sidewalk, paving, picnic table, street lamp, in that rough circle that touches the Lodge, and then the Community Center, a former lab building—postwar, second-generation, built in concrete; the hundred-foot diameter Pond now banded by a neat cement sidewalk; and the Los Alamos County Building, which looks like a high-flying savings and loan from the early seventies. And then our farmers' market of some twenty to fifty pickups and station wagons that assemble in a roughly oval form in the pine trees, on the sloping ground, from around six in the morning each summer Thursday. The little gathering completes the circle, an area of perhaps five or six acres, one of those nodes of extraordinary historical intensity which is belied by the apparent calm and even peacefulness of the present-day site.

The passer-through could miss it all. The sheltered brass plaque on the far side of the Pond. The tiny Historical Museum next to the Lodge, a kind of shrine to the good old days of total secrecy (*pace* David Greenglass and Klaus Fuchs)—or the illusion of it. And your standard innocent would know little or none of this. He or she could drive across this expanse in ten seconds, see nothing. "What, the atomic bomb was invented here?"

Twenty years ago I was such an innocent, breathlessly driving my VW van toward the legendary laboratory salvage yard in search of bargains—or whatever you call the expensive-looking debris that sells by the pound, which enthusiastic scavengers believe surely can be made useful again. I was young or youngish, I had a wife and child, I was going to build a house, which meant that I had license to become a pack rat. Those first visits yielded some wide redwood boards, one of which I still use for various purposes, and other odds and ends that have since blended into the landscape. My desk is spotted with demobilized or outmoded office fixtures from Los Alamos. The chair I sit on to write

[218]

once served the back and bottom of some laboratory physicist or bureaucrat or flunky. And for years I banged away on a giant wide-carriage Royal that had, by all evidence, been little-used before being sold for a tenth of its value.

My first memory of the atomic bomb connects to something other than Hiroshima and Nagasaki. I was seven in the summer of 1945, probably too young to understand what adults were having to learn about and imagine among themselves. News of the end of the war in Europe came over the radio. It meant that my mother had hope of eventually receiving word of her father in Stuttgart. I was home sick from school that day. My mother let me go out in my bathrobe into the dark garage and sit at the wheel of our green Ford sedan and honk the horn. But for VJ day several months later, the Japanese surrender, there's a blank in my memory.

A couple of years later a breakfast cereal company began selling through the mail a toy called the atomic bomb ring. It followed a long line of Captain Midnight and Superman rings which featured magical emblems or secret compartments or compasses or magnets. They were brass-plated pot metal and plastic creations advertised on the evening radio serials and the backs of breakfast-food packages. To obtain one, you had to send in a quarter or thirty-five cents and a box top or coupon. The first kid to get one in the mail commanded waves of interest at school for a day or two, until the flimsy plastic fittings broke or until the varnish wore off the brass plating to leave a greenish band on your sweaty finger.

The atomic bomb ring represented a startling departure in the ring market from the usual hidden compartments and emblems. It consisted of a bullet-shaped form about the size of a .22 cartridge, mounted atop a brass ring, with a finned red plastic cap that covered a tiny lens. You were supposed to step inside a darkened room and hold the lens to your eye until you saw dimly pulsating greenish spots. The ring cost a dollar, a large sum for a middle-class nine-year-old.

I dutifully taped my four shiny quarters to a piece of shirt board and mailed it off. But the ring didn't arrive in the expected month or six weeks, a blow to my status at school—where Kip and Jimmy were parading their atomic bomb rings up and down the covered boardwalk that ran alongside the classrooms, until Kip lost his down the wide cracks between the boards. The school had been hastily built late in the war. Shortages dictated that the porch boards be laid not side by side but with lumber-saving gaps which also happened to be wide enough to consume coins, pencils, and atomic bomb rings. Fishing out lost items was a regular recess pastime.

My mother finally sat down and wrote a letter to the atomic bomb ring people demanding satisfaction for her disappointed boy. Not long after that I became aware of the fact that at least one adult in the family circle regarded the ring as controversial when he forbade his daughter Rowena to order it. This was a new and interesting breeze crossing my world; I made note of it without having any idea of its meaning. Eventually my atomic bomb ring arrived. In all I probably spent no more than a few minutes staring into its lens in my closet among boxes cluttered with electric trains, or in the hall closet with the vacuum cleaner, pushing aside overcoats no one ever seemed to wear. I probably lost the red lens cap too, and my finger started turning green, and the ring ended up in a box of childhood treasures of the sort that time speedily devalues.

It seems strange now that a toy introduced me to the nuclear age, but then that is what toys also do: they carry the news in the coded way of all artifacts. This was the first message I was to receive from Los Alamos, sent by way of various intermediaries all struggling to imagine and represent a new element of civilization.

As a freshman at the University of Chicago, one of my classes was in the basement of the West Stands next to a green-painted space, aquarium-like, illuminated by sunlight reaching down from windows set at sidewalk level, where Enrico Fermi had created the first sustained nuclear reaction only eleven years before—though it seemed a lifetime then for this particular seventeen-year-old.

There followed the usual experience of the fifties and sixties, by the end of which I was protesting the war in Vietnam by marching in the streets. That war was comprehensible in its way and arguably wrong, while the Cold War and the nuclear arms race seemed more like a disease, a systemic pathology of the body politic with no known cure. I spent the seventies turning away from it all to raise children, build a house, grow garlic.

In March 1982 I received a visit from a federal investigator seeking background information on a woman who had recently worked for us on the farm. The visit would have been innocuous had I not just returned from a long walk in which I was puzzling through my inability to write a chapter about Los Alamos for a book I didn't yet know I would never finish—tentative conclusion being that I was largely ignorant of Los Alamos even though it was only an hour's drive away and even though it was where most of my neighbors and a couple of friends worked, and where—had I forgotten?—I had done a brief stint as a technical writing consultant for a solar project around 1972. The security investigator was oddly terrified at our dogs, and I was afraid of him; but the interview proceeded politely if a little strainedly; and no, Orlina didn't drink, didn't use drugs, had surely never belonged to any subversive organizations, she was one of the nicest people in the universe—which she happens to be. But inwardly I raged. What is this, 1954? Subversive organizations? I thought they had long ago stopped asking these questions. I had visions of security investigators plying the villages and towns of northern New Mexico, the schools, the offices, the businesses, asking their questions again and again, year after year, turning neighbors and friends and relatives into informers and snitches. I could not call this a police state, but I could call it a functional blueprint for a police state should one be found to be politically expedient; the machinery is there for keeping track of large numbers of people and for making everybody believe that it's for the larger good, which is the better part of the substance of any such apparatus.

But true, I could forget that the money I had saved twenty years before to go to Europe and become a novelist had been earned as a technical writer for a missile firm, and that once I had filled out all those forms, and that once I had worn a badge to work, that I had had a secret clearance, that at the nadir of that experience I had been asked to show films (having skills as a projectionist) for a chemical-biological warfare conference, to project in the early morning hours U.S. Government Savings Bond commercials centered around gruesome clips of Fidel Castro's firing squads, inspiring government contractors to invest in their ultimate employer.

I can't say why I stopped being a believer, perhaps then, in a cold sweat in the dark auditorium of Norton Air Force Base. Later, surely, I became weary of the leverage of fear that the arms race exerted on all who could bear to think of it.

The winter after the federal investigator's visit, the winter of 1982–83, the next writing season, I spent a day a week up in Los Alamos poking around. I went alone some days, took friends with me on others. I read in the Lab's vast technical library, the two floors of it open to the public, I ate in the cafeteria with its stunning view of the Sangre de Cristos, I drove around the public roads of the Laboratory grounds, I went to the Science Museum, the Los Alamos Historical Museum, talked to friends who lived there or had once lived there, I looked at street maps and Geological Survey maps, Laboratory maps and environmental impact studies, drove around Los Alamos and down into its bedroom suburb of White Rock, week after week; I read novels set in Los Alamos, articles about the town, watched TV documentaries, read through histories and memoirs.

But I was no journalist. I had no head for the scientific and technical intricacies. I was too partisan. I was sure all those around would hear the axe grinding in my questions and remarks. At the center of it all was death, the vast inescapable fact that this was a tunnel into which one would enter with little hope of seeing any light again: nuclear weapons were supreme instruments of death and destruction, and there was no way I could think of them as anything else.

And this was what I had moved within forty-five miles of, this was where Rose Mary and I had built our house of mud bricks, this was where we were raising our children, this was where we had made our little garlic farm: on the lee side, downwind, of the radiant brain of the nuclear arms race.

The Los Alamos National Laboratory is a big place. A billion dollars gets zapped, boiled, cooked, banged, boomed, copied, faxed, fiddled, stolen and given away up there every year. Seven thousand men and women think and calculate and scheme and lobby and write studies and conduct tests and adjustments, build things and tear them down, radiate everything in sight and then try to de-radiate it, invent and dis-invent, eat lunch, jog, play volleyball, receive regular paychecks and generous benefits up there every year, as they have for nearly fifty years now, as they plan to for the next fifty years as well.

This is why I sell garlic and flowers at the farmers' market in Los Alamos. On the gravel, in the pines, a stone's throw from where Oppenheimer and his colleagues thought out the details of the Hiroshima and Nagasaki bombs.

You may say that the place gives you the creeps. I understand. It once made me angry to the point of speechlessness. And true, if some scientist or engineer or janitor presses the wrong button in the Plutonium Facility across the canyon a mile from where I sit on the back of my tailgate with my onions and garlic and basil, I'm a goner as surely as most of the city of ten thousand—or much of northern New Mexico, for that matter. This is alarmist conjecture, to be sure. But there's much secrecy at the Lab, which no doubt allows for a lot of sloppiness and for bad science or non-science masquerading as science, secrecy which generally makes it impossible for anyone to accurately assess the risks of selling flowers a mile downwind from the Plutonium Facility or growing garlic forty-five miles downwind either.

Creepy, yes, in that sense. I used to take naps on the grass next to the Pond after the market until I realized what had been there in the late 1940s and early 1950s. Then I decided it might be more prudent despite the heat to take naps inside the cab of the truck. But not creepy in the other sense, of inventing diabolical machinery. What I came to understand was that the United States of America is the biggest gun-runner in the history of the world. We've armed ourselves privately and publicly to the teeth and armed the rest of the world as well: for the past fifty years we've invented, tested, manufactured, distributed untold billions in armaments. Besides being used in the wars we ourselves have fought, the guns and bombs we make have largely served to make repressive governments even more repressive, simply because governments are better customers for armaments than individuals, except perhaps in the USA. Which is to say that there is an inherently authoritarian, anti-democratic bias to virtually all weapons work.

Los Alamos is where the best bangs are invented. You can hear some of the smaller tests going off in the arroyos at noon. Yet in this work you may argue that it's unfair to single out for criticism Los Alamos or the Department of Energy or the University of California, manager of the Lab, because so much of this work is carried out in virtually every major city in the country.

This as I say is why I sell garlic in Los Alamos. The place is really no worse than anywhere else. And in many respects as a community it is far better than most: wonderful views, clear air, good schools, no crime (in the usual sense of the word), fine libraries, excellent swimming pool, mountain walks and skiing just up the hill. And you can argue that its citizens have fewer illusions about the central business of the nation, to develop and manufacture the world's best weapons. Elsewhere it's much easier to turn your back, go about your own private little business, pay your taxes, trust in the wisdom of those who guide our nation, and believe that all is well.

But in Los Alamos the question must be constantly addressed or excused, or rationalized, or put aside, because it so constantly forces its way into view in the large and small ways of any town. If you want to know what military socialism looks like, come to Los Alamos. If you want to know what the future could look like for all of us—supposing the nation finally acknowledges its continuing interest in supplying arms for all the world's dictators and all the world's wars—then Los Alamos is a place you ought to have a look at.

I don't find it creepy anymore. I've been up there hundreds of times. I can drive by the lights and storage tanks and towers of the old Plutonium Facility across from the airport and wonder calmly how many hundreds of years will be needed to complete its decontamination. I can glance to the right at the runway that parallels the highway into town, see if the Ross Airlines turboprop is in yet, and I can recall reading that they stopped flying plutonium in and out of Los Alamos twenty years ago—or so they say, because how would we know otherwise? I can turn right at the Lodge, once part of a school, now home of the Chamber of Commerce, a place where meetings and wedding receptions are held, and think of the stroke of malign genius fifty years ago that led our universities into the business of inventing weapons of mass destruction. I can wonder if they will ever be able to redeem themselves from this philosophical betrayal.

My intention when I first decided to sell my garlic up there was to stop being afraid of Los Alamos. My intention was to become part of the place, to experience it, to earn a point of view about it, as one who to a certain extent had made Los Alamos his community too.

My point of view is the tailgate of my pickup, parked each Thursday morning in summer on the rim of that five-acre circle within which was invented a half-century ago the first atomic bombs. My customers are the women and men of Los Alamos, some of whom were there at the beginning, and their sons and daughters, and their successors, the wives of their successors, who carry on the work begun in 1943, and their grandchildren, and their great-grandchildren who sweep through the market area in little bands on excursions from day-care centers.

They are good customers. I cannot think of them as evil people. We've got to know each other in a polite, distant way over the past seven or eight years I've been selling there. We chat a lot about gardens, and the weather, and how to cook this and that. We don't talk about all the rest. Los Alamos people seem slow to accept outsiders, perhaps fearing what they think of Los Alamos. But I know how to speak their language. The first time I come up to Los Alamos each season, it feels like going home to the Southern California of the fifties and sixties. Most of the farmers who sell in Los Alamos are Hispanic. Most of the customers are Anglo women. As an Anglo male with a university education, I'm on the wrong side of the wooden planks and apple boxes that make up my stand. But my customers have decided I'm all right.

In fact I'm not. But since I'm part of the place, perhaps certain things are being overlooked. I worried about my business when a little group I belong to, the Los Alamos Study Group, decided to meet at Fuller Lodge once a month on Sunday evenings to discuss so many of those things people in northern New Mexico are afraid of or reluctant to talk about. We decided to announce our topics in the local paper, and give our names in an ad we paid for ourselves. Over the course of several months a handful of Los Alamos people came to our meetings and joined in our thoughtful discussions—a handful of potentially thousands. Perhaps those others were worried about their jobs, just as I was worried about my business. But the greatest danger of all in a country that prides itself on being a democracy is failing to speak your mind, to speak your fears and worries, to risk your job, your business.

Los Alamos has never figured out how to monumentalize itself, a ticklish problem for the city known as the destroyer of cities. Oppenheimer was perhaps drawn to northern New Mexico by the same spell of the landscape that lured later generations of artists and anarchists to the region, to paint, to write, to build houses of mud, grow garlic. Perhaps he was conscious of the fact that he was founding high in the mountains a modern Delphi. He fished for imagery in mystical literature and came up with a line from a sonnet by John Donne for the name of the first atomic test in Alamogordo, which eventually became the name of the main drag of the town, Trinity Drive. Betrayed by his friends and vilified by the times, his ghost had to be long content with a truncated one-way street off Trinity in his name, whose principal address was the police department, and with an annual lecture series in his honor. Not until 1983 did the Lab pay official homage when it renamed the library after its founder.

The bombs are there, of course, in the Bradbury Science Museum, less a museum than a public relations shrine, and named after Oppenheimer's successor—whose wife buys my onions and garlic. The bombs or rather their replicas are painted white, but without the graffiti the bomber crews scribbled all over them as they were loaded into their planes, which we would now regard as tasteless, and are without the red spray paint lines along the steel joints. But in their whiteness they are more realistic than the sinister black shapes on display at the National Atomic Museum in Albuquerque, a true cathedral, or Lourdes, or Disneyland, of the nuclear arms race.

Nor do the names of the several hundred streets of the town reflect its history except in perhaps three or four cases, Oppenheimer Drive of course, Manhattan Drive, and Trinity Drive. In this largely Anglo town most of the rest are in Real

Estate Spanish, a commercial dialect that extends across much of the Southwest.

And in fact what monument could you erect to commemorate the grand achievement of this town and its famous national laboratory, arguably one of the most powerful places on earth?

As I sit on my tailgate in the pines, my back to the grassy clearing, I sometimes think about the rough circle of trees and grass and pavement ringed by the Historical Museum and Lodge and Community Center, the round crater-like Pond, County Building, and farmers' market: here perhaps is that monument, a grassy space a few acres in extent, without prominent stone or marker.

It is a space to which I come once a week in the summer with my flowers and garlic. It would not do to call them offerings or charms. I am not a believer in the simplistic evils, in vampires.

Yet all this vaguely—disjointedly—adds up to why I choose to sell in Los Alamos, and why I persist in this exchange. I am pleased when a bureaucrat or engineer or scientist from the Lab comes by the market early in the morning and buys up an armload of bouquets for his secretarial staff back at the office, over to the west, across the canyon, over the bridge, behind the guarded doors. It pleases me to think of those flowers making their way into the inner recesses of a place most Americans will be forever forbidden to visit.

※

38

MIRACLE CURE

THIS BRINGS US back to where we started: planting, in the ground, a clove at a time, any side up, in September or October.

There's a previous step I haven't mentioned, which is breaking up the bulbs into cloves, and it takes almost as long as planting. For a few rows, it is not a big job, but when you've got three or four hundred pounds to deal with then you're facing a major task.

Top-setting garlic offers a slight advantage here in that the stalk can be used to help open up the bulb and crack it in half, the hardest step of the process. Top-setting bulbs are also lacking the inner ring of sliver-like cloves which are difficult to separate and arguably too small to plant. Once the bulb is split open you must then separate a dozen or more cloves from each other one at a time; often there are a few large cloves to which a smaller one cleaves tightly, and these must be pried apart. The work must be done gently with fingers and nails so as to inflict as little damage as possible to the tender cloves.

If storage conditions have been somewhat damp you will see the nubbins of first root growth swelling and lengthening at the base of each clove. The tiny fingers may even serve to push the cloves away from the rooting base of the seed stalk, that inverted umbrella-like form which, along with layers of skin enwrapping the bulb, holds the cloves together, and often so firmly that the germ breaks off the end of cloves when you tear the bulb apart. The hard root base serves to shield this most sensitive part of the clove from injuries while being handled. Later in the season, in autumn, the tight bond between clove and root base begins to loosen, and bulb can be broken apart without tearing away the base of the cloves.

In breaking up bulbs virtually every clove needs to pass through your fingers, as in planting itself. If the bulbs are large, breaking up goes relatively rapidly. Clove by clove, buckets and lug boxes fill to the snapping sound of bulbs being twisted open, the rustling noise of skin falling away, of cloves dropping into plastic buckets. Three or four of us will work at breaking up, out in the afternoon sun, hunching over our receptacles and ringed by piles of roots and white and purple skin. Once full of broken-up cloves, lug boxes go back into the cool of the shed until we're ready to plant. The work invariably does violence to a certain number of cloves; it should take place close to planting time so that injured cloves will quickly rejoin the damp earth, an ideal medium for their healing.

But the task is long and often we need to start several weeks in advance. This is occasioned by the annual visit of my eighty-year-old parents. Since her stroke, breaking up garlic has become increasingly important for my mother: it offers a task for two weeks out of the year at which she can work like everyone else, in a corner of the garlic shed where she sits with a lug box on her lap and sorts through the bulbs and feels out the ones that need to be broken up. She was always a great lover of garlic since long before it was fashionable to admit such tastes; and perhaps the yearly labor conjures up as well the beds of daffodil and ranunculi, whose bulbs she used to plant down by the stream beneath the sycamores.

It takes us about sixty working hours to break up and plant

our 120 rows of garlic, our acre and a half, time that is spread through September and October and sometimes into the first weeks of November. Garlic left over from planting goes into Rose Mary's arrangements for the shop and for an annual open house the village hosts the first weekend of November, when we also sell off the last of the market grade except for a few lug boxes we set aside for ourselves for the winter.

By mid-November we're down to a few boxes stored under old sleeping bags in the back of the shed. Our planted rows will be working at the quiet business of rooting in the damp earth. Here and there they'll send up the odd shoot into the cool air to explore the waning light. We'll use our stored garlic in salads and sauces, on bread, and in almost every cooked dish. When either of us comes down with a cold or whenever someone walks into the house complaining of one, Rose Mary will chop up a couple of cloves and prescribe them to be swallowed without chewing—to reduce the odor on the breath.

Her enthusiasm has always been a great healer. And perhaps the garlic helps. My files are crammed with newspaper articles claiming as much. In a creeping way scientific studies seem to be confirming the folk wisdom that has claimed much good of the plant for thousands of years.

But health is never simply an individual matter. Your own health is inextricably tied to that of your family, your friends, that of your community, your nation, your environment, your Earth. What you put in your mouth will be only an incomplete fragment of a whole, and to complete that whole you should have a hand in growing some portion of what you eat. Garlic may be good for you. But growing your own garlic may be even better.

The food you grow yourself will always be better for you than food produced by utter strangers and distant corporations, which will be guided by goals other than an intimate concern for your own good health.

Now and then a customer will approach our stand at the farmers' market and tell me how much garlic he or she goes through in a day, how many cloves, how many bulbs. I usually express approval. Perhaps I am envied as one who keeps a ton or more on hand through much of the year.

But fortunately for my business I'm not a great eater of garlic, at least in its unadulterated form. I'm never pleased to discover a slice of raw clove in a mouthful of salad. I find it painful to down those chopped-up cloves Rose Mary promises will cure my cold. I am, however, a great eater of it in cooked form, she assures me, in pastas and casseroles, probably consuming much more than I am aware of.

My aversion to the raw clove perhaps says only that the filaments of memory and passion that weave grower to plant are not exclusively linked to taste buds. And even that a certain distance here may allow me to appreciate the whole plant, its cycles, its place in my life as an organizing principle, in ways perhaps that a gourmet consumer of the bulb may be indifferent to, along with the other elaborate processes which convey the bulb to the chopping block.

You pay homage when and where you can. I love the smell of the bulb as the earth opens and releases it in harvest, an aroma that only those who grow garlic and handle the bulb and the leaves still fresh from the earth can know. It is a smell richer and more vibrant and expansive than what most people think of as garlic. Anyone who gardens knows these indescribable presences—of not only fresh garlic, but onions, carrots and their tops, parsley's piercing signal, the fragrant exultations of a tomato plant in its prime, sweet explosions of basil. They can be known best and most purely on the spot, in the instant, in the garden, in the sun, in the rain. They cannot be carried away from their place in the earth. They are inimitable. And they have no shelf life at all.

39

FINANCIAL STATEMENT

THE QUESTION HAS been asked: "Do you actually make a living on an acre and a half of garlic?"

No: it takes another acre of statice flowers and two or three acres of vegetables, mainly winter squash and pumpkins, to make a living.

A strictly financial view of the farm is what I have to take during the annual accounting with the Farmers Home Administration at the end of each year, in the declining days of early December. The frames of my farm life contract to the partitions and fixtures of a standard government-issue office in a nearby town, and to the dollar value of what Rose Mary and I produce and to our costs and expenses. The fields are a memory now, the shadows are cold, and in the dry, overheated air of an office my farm life could seem to take place on another planet.

There is an element of luck in all economic arrangements, which has to do with whether the tides of economic change happen to be going with or against your own personal inclinations. Our balance sheet often looks good because the four acres we bought in the 1970s have appreciated markedly; and because we built our house with our own hands as money became available, we have never been burdened with a mortgage. We're fortunate to live in a region where we can retail the vast bulk of what we grow. The occasional good farming year has made up for a few bad years, and literary advances and grants, extended family loans, low-interest FmHA loans, short-term operating loans from a local bank have enabled us to keep going; consequently our short- and medium-term debts are reasonable in relation to our assets.

But the frames of the conventional financial statement are narrow. They tend to leave out which way the economic tide is moving, thus excluding important shifts in the attribution of costs and in the creation of value. Over the past ten years, for people at the lower end of the economic scale the tide withdrew in the form of rising health care and education costs and reduced levels of social services in general, while an ever-increasing share of public wealth flowed to the military-industrial complex, and into a vast nonproductive sector of financial manipulation—with its grotesque transfers of wealth and debt. This state of affairs is reflected in the disparity between those at the bottom earning a minimum wage with few or no fringe benefits, and the fortunes paid those at the pinnacle of professional and corporate structures. This is a weight that bears down on the negative side of our balance sheet as much as it does on that of anyone at the lower and least-structured end of the economic scale.

By opening up the frame, we can include other factors which do not fit into the boxes and lines of the usual financial statement. There is the fact that my labor and Rose Mary's provide food for ourselves and our friends and workers, and that it is of greater nutritional value than most supermarket produce. Further, I regard our labor as a product, not an expense: it is healthy in itself, at least much of the time, which means that we place a lesser burden on the health care system than we might were we working in a polluted city at more lucrative occupations.

The farm also enables us to contribute time and money to two local acequias and the farmers' markets, thereby adding value to the infrastructure of our village and to neighboring towns. There is no place on the financial statement for this value.

And in such community work, and through the farm, we're able to live out our passion for this land, its skies, its waters. We're able to shape and nourish and maintain a landscape, as tenders of irrigation channels and watchers of rivers, as stewards of the small parcels of land that have fallen under our care.

The wealth that comes to us from the earth is considerable, however undervalued it may be in the marketplace. Even when we think ourselves strapped or poor, most years we're able to contribute hundreds of pounds of produce, even tons, to those far more in need than ourselves. Whatever produce spoils goes into the compost heap or into the goose pen, to return eventually to feed the earth again. Thus we burden no landfill or sewage treatment plant with farm wastes or kitchen scraps.

Security can be seen as a complex of investments in real estate, stocks and bonds, retirement plans, life insurance, health plans, and so on. Or it can be defined as that web of arrangements with family and friends and neighbors and coworkers, and with the land itself, which one has woven into a sense of community. We have virtually no institutional security of the conventional sort: we have chosen instead to place our security in the hands of the community in which we live and work. Such is the old way, the traditional way; and who knows, this old way may be more certain than its institutional counterpart, particularly in a time of failing banks and insurance companies and evasive governmental agencies.

Toward the end of each year, when the financial accounting is over and done with in the Farmers Home Administration office, and I am back home fretting over the always-unsatisfactory numbers, I will often pose the question in an extreme form: Would I rather have a substantial savings account, a health plan, life insurance, a pension plan—yet hate the life I lead in order to have these things? We have chosen to make a living, not endure one. In the deeper sense, ends mostly meet—perhaps as much as they ever do in human life.

The shadows are long, and the numbers are always unsatisfactory, and when the forms are filled out and the account books closed the winter looms ahead as a cold tunnel down into which one must descend. But there are the little flames. The catalogs arrive with their bright pictures of fruits and flowers and of astoundingly perfect heads of lettuce. And with them, the hope, the determination that next year the same mistakes won't be made, that the weather will be better, without drought or flood or hail or frosts too late or too early, that next year I'll be stronger, wiser, more foresighted, more philosophical, more pragmatic; perhaps less idealistic, perhaps less the dreamer.

But who knows. Perhaps I perversely enjoy making the same mistakes over and over again—perhaps I even take a wry pleasure in seeing what new ones I can come up with after all this time, because there will always be new ones. Of course the cycle is flawed. There can be no perfection, only dreams of it, dreams of improvement, ease, completion.

Yet the dream must have its day, it must have its hour, its season to rebuild the little hearth where hopes may glow and flame, its private space where it can weave to its own pattern the commercial imaginings of the greater world, which wishes to do all your dreaming for you, your imagining, and which will try to form and reform your hopes to its own ends. The dream is a labor both of self-creation but also of self-defense against the commercial imagination of our time, whose boundless resources are so artfully beamed into those spaces we think of as our own, and which would harness our needs and desires and fears and fantasies to their profitable ends: free enterprise, so called, knows no bounds and shrinks from no means in the pursuit of its power over the imagination.

Thus to dream a garden and then to plant it is an act of independence and even defiance to that greater world. And though that garden or field you have first dreamed and then planted may later come in the high summer noon to seem a tyranny of its own, it is nonetheless one to which you have bound yourself voluntarily, with eyes open, head clear, without intermediary, without the sleight of hand and the duplicity, or with much less of them, of human aggregations—political, corporate, whatever—that will always aspire to feed you, fuel your equipment, illuminate your nights, and imagine away your life.

The dreams will fail. There is no perfection. There will be drought, flood, plague—inevitably, everywhere, sooner, then later again. But everywhere also the imagination will overcome them, and like the spider that within hours emerges from the rubble to spin a first silver filament across the desert created by a man on an orange tractor as he tills under the last harvested field, it will begin its work of creation and re-creation. It has not—you may argue—yet been wholly defeated anywhere. It may, for all its sloppiness and foolishness, be our most powerful faculty.

FINANCIAL STATEMENT

The numbers are quickly forgotten. The financial statement must finally give way to the narrative, with all its exceptions, special cases, imponderables. It must finally give way to the story, which is perhaps the way we arm ourselves against the next and always unpredictable turn of the cycle in the quixotic dare that is life: across the rock and cold of lifelessness, it is our seed, our clove, our filament cast toward the future.

＊

SOURCES

UNTIL RECENTLY, the only general text that treated garlic in any detail was the long out-of-print *Onions and Their Allies* by Henry Albert Jones and Louis K. Mann, Interscience Publishers, New York, 1963. In the fall of 1991, however, Ron Engeland published his *Growing Great Garlic,* Filaree Productions, Okanogan, WA (see Filaree Farms address below).

The Garlic Seed Foundation of New York State, Rose Valley Farm, Rose, NY 14542-0149, publishes the *Garlic Press,* a newsletter of interest to small-scale garlic growers.

The Gilroy Garlic Festival takes place each year at the end of July; contact the Gilroy (California) Chamber of Commerce for more information.

The Fresh Garlic Association, PO Box 2410, Sausalito, CA 94966, publishes a promotional newsletter called the *Fresh Garlic News*.

Filaree Farm, Rt. 1, Box 162, Okanogan, WA 98840, is actively engaged in classifying and cataloguing various garlic cultivars from around the world and making these available in small quantities for trial plantings.

The following firms offer specialty varieties of garlic:

ALLIUM FARMS
Box 296
Powers, OR 97466

FISH LAKE GARLIC MAN
RR 2
Demorestville, Ont.
Canada K0K 1W0

KALMIA FARMS
PO Box 3881
Charlottesville, VA 22903

LIBBY CREEK FARM
PO Box 177
Carlton, WA 98814

For large plantings, a commercial supplier of California Early and California Late varieties is the Joseph Gubser Company, PO Box 427, Gilroy, CA 95021.

For equipment for the small grower, I have found these two firms particularly helpful: Ferrari Tractor, PO Box 1045, Gridley, CA 95948; and Market Farm Implement, RD #2, Box 206, Friedens, PA 15541. Eversman, Inc., PO Box 390336, Denver, CO 80239, manufactures "Spinsweeps" for undercutting garlic and onions; and the Ventura Manufacturing and Implement Company makes one- and two-row garlic planters available through Ferrari Tractor or Market Farm Implement or other distributors.

English Men of Letters

EDITED BY JOHN MORLEY

GRAY